WHAT PEOPLE ARE

# WILL YOU JOIN IN (

This is a book for anyone who has ever watched *Les Misérables* – and most of us have! It's gloriously, refreshingly different; fascinating on many levels; but above all deeply helpful. I don't think I ever enjoyed a devotional book more than this one!
**Jennifer Rees Larcombe**, Christian author and Speaker

An excellent resource! Steve Mann's captivating reflections masterfully intertwine Victor Hugo's narrative with practical and inspiring Bible study, unpacking powerful Christian themes. Steve effectively encourages readers to observe God's Spirit at work through the struggles of the characters in *Les Miserables*, helping us to reflect on our own lives and the world we live in. Buy this book, study it, and enjoy a veritable feast for Lent!
**Tony Miles**, presenter for Premier Christian Radio and contributor to 'Pause for Thought', BBC Radio 2

The pressing challenge for the Church is to tell the story, God's story, in an accessible way. In Victor Hugo's story *Les Misérables* Steve Mann has found a way of weaving the two stories together to great effect.

If you have been enthralled, excited and challenged by the strong Christian message in *Les Misérables*, if you want to understand the God story better, help others hear it in a fresh way, and find ways to apply it in daily life, then this devotional book is for you.

I warmly commend it as a resource for Christians to deepen their discipleship and to more effectively live out their faith.
**The Revd Canon John Carne**, Former Chair of the Plymouth & Exeter Methodist District

Victor Hugo's epic novel has been enjoyed by readers and now

moviegoers alike. Yet a deeper subtext of understanding is woven through Hugo's words. Betrayal, forgiveness, faith, hope and love are all themes shared by both the biblical text and by *Les Misérables*. Revd Steve Mann masterfully navigates the spiritual and biblical themes of Hugo's work, drawing the reader into a world where day-to-day spirituality meets 19th-century France and reaches forward into our hearts and minds even still – reminding us that, "To love another person is to see the face of God."
**Revd Mike Rayson**, OSL, Senior Pastor, Bethalto United Methodist Church

The screen version if the classic *Les Miserables* has brought this fascinating book to wide attention again. It is full of the themes of human endurance, sacrifice, forgiveness and redemption. Through this series of Bible Studies and reflections Steve Mann helps us to look again at the gospel narratives of the ministry of Jesus and discover how his death and resurrection can shape and transform our lives. I warmly commend this timely book for use in small groups and private study.
**John Hellyer**, Chair of the South East Methodist District

# Will You Join in Our Crusade?

The invitation of the Gospels unlocked by
the inspiration of *Les Misérables*
A seven-week course for Lent or anytime

# Will You Join in Our Crusade?

The invitation of the Gospels unlocked by
the inspiration of *Les Misérables*
A seven-week course for Lent or anytime

Steve Mann

Circle Books

Winchester, UK
Washington, USA

First published by Circle Books, 2013
Circle Books is an imprint of John Hunt Publishing Ltd., Laurel House, Station Approach,
Alresford, Hants, SO24 9JH, UK
office1@jhpbooks.net
www.johnhuntpublishing.com
www.circle-books.com

For distributor details and how to order please visit the 'Ordering' section on our website.

Text copyright: Steve Mann 2013

ISBN: 978 1 78279 384 7

A CIP catalogue record for this book is available from the British Library.

Design: Lee Nash

Printed and bound by CPI Group (UK) Ltd, Croydon, CR0 4YY

We operate a distinctive and ethical publishing philosophy in all areas of our business, from our global network of authors to production and worldwide distribution.

# CONTENTS

*There are families, but there is nothing of the sort for me. I am an unlucky wretch; I am left outside. Did I have a father and mother? I almost doubt it.*

Jean Valjean

*To Karen, Tim and Euan*
*– The greatest family a man could ever wish for.*

# Introduction

In the customary excess of the world we live in the word 'phenomenon' is regularly over-used. Yet, in the case of the musical *Les Misérables*, it seems well-justified. It has played to tens of millions of people worldwide since its first performance in 1980 and, translated to the silver screen, virtuoso performances from the likes of Hugh Jackman, Anne Hathaway and Russell Crowe saw it garner three Oscars at the 2013 Academy Awards. This success becomes all the more remarkable given that the musical's subject matter originates from a vast, sometimes rambling, French language book published in 1862. What usually happens is that such works become more and more obscure until they drop off the horizons of all but the very literary. Why then does this story continue to capture so many hearts?

Some 2000 years ago, a carpenter's son from Nazareth stood in his hometown synagogue and read from what we now know as the Old Testament book of Isaiah. *"The Spirit of the Lord is on me, because he has anointed me to proclaim good news to the poor. He has sent me to proclaim freedom for the prisoners and recovery of sight for the blind, to set the oppressed free, to proclaim the year of the Lord's favor."* He added: *"Today this scripture is fulfilled in your hearing."* (Luke 4:18-21).

His message was simple. Jesus envisaged a society in which all wrongs would be righted because his God would be at the center. His Spirit-empowered role was to make it possible for that new world to come into being. Incidentally, you've probably worked out from the Bible passage above that Jesus' God wasn't the hard, nasty, punishing kind of god. His God was full of understanding love and restoring grace. Just the kind of god you couldn't help but like if you bumped into them at a party!

Jesus invited people to realign their mindsets and lifestyles in order to bear witness to this new way of being. He called them to be disciples, people who would commit their lives to him; learn from him and put his ideas into practice. His undying belief in those ideas would lead him to the cross but also to an ultimate vindication of his vision. And his parting words were for his disciples to continue their mission by going global; spreading the message of discipleship and teaching others as Jesus had taught them.

Why are people so captivated by *Les Misérables*? Could it be that, at its heart, it's nothing less than the dream articulated by Jesus. As we enter into Valjean's struggles to conscientiously live a new life. As we rejoice to see his role as protector of the poor and downtrodden. As we weep at the cruelties heaped upon Fantine by uncaring people. As we resonate with the students' ideal of a better world to come. Are we not simply seeing the world through God's eyes and connecting with the God-given hope planted within us and all humanity?

Let me make you a confession. I am not normally a great fan of musicals; nor of French literature. The only reason I went to see the musical, back in 2006, was because my son was taking part in a school production. Like many others I came away a convert. Not only was I humming all the melodies but a Christian message seemed to leap out from virtually every line. Soon, I was working through the unabridged English translation of the book (which weighs in at well over 1000 pages). Not surprisingly, I found much that had been omitted in order to keep the musical to a manageable length but again the Christian themes, so evident in the musical, were there before me. My reading spread through the days leading up to Good Friday and the story seemed a perfect complement to the retelling of those familiar events from Jesus' life.

A three-month sabbatical followed the following year, the fruits of which you now have before you. In writing this book I have sought to let *Les Misérables* and the Gospels spark off one another in the conviction that, at heart, they are one and the same story. My prayer is that *Les Misérables* does for you as much as it has for me.

Steve Mann
https://www.facebook.com/joininourcrusade
https://www.joininourcrusade.com

# How to use this book

There are two ways to use this resource:

(1) If you wish to use the book specifically for Lent then begin on Ash Wednesday and finish on Easter Sunday. The final two days then become optional extras. (2) Otherwise, the book can be enjoyed as a seven-week course at any time of year, to be started on whichever day you choose.

At its heart is a 42-day devotional reading plan that will take you through the entirety of Victor Hugo's classic novel. Each day begins with a Gospel passage and will require five to ten minutes of your time. Use whichever version of the Bible you feel comfortable with for these readings. You may find it helpful to keep a pen and paper close by in order to note down any thoughts or questions that arise. Is any prior knowledge of *Les Misérables* needed? No. The readings will give you all you need to build up the story in chronological order but, if you do get the chance to read the book/watch the musical/see the movie before you start, then this won't go amiss.

The material is also grouped around seven themes at the heart of Christian experience: Week 1 – Grace, Week 2 – Responsibility, Week 3 – Truth, Week 4 – Compassion, Week 5 – Fellowship, Week 6 – Darkness, Week 7 – Reconciliation.

Every seventh day takes a break from reading and contains questions for group discussion or personal reflection. If you are undertaking the course as a group, it should lead to a meeting between one and two hours long, dependent upon your size and talkativeness.

The weekly questions follow a pattern. This begins with *Setting the Scene*, an opportunity to follow some of the action from the DVD of the 2012 movie release. Mostly, this stays very close to Victor Hugo's original. Be aware, though, that there are times when events and characters from the novel are considerably

4

adapted or even omitted altogether. Don't worry if you do not have a copy of the DVD. Just move on to the next section.

There are two sections that bear the title *i2i* ('eye to eye'). The first – 'issues to explore' and 'irritants' – follows *Setting the Scene*. The second – 'insights' and 'implementation' – comes at the end of each session. The idea behind each is that members of a group sharing this journey are there to support one another. This is important both in making sense of our initial responses to the material but also in helping each other grow from the experience. My hope is that the first of these sections will prompt plenty of discussion. Remember that the things we react against can often be as illuminating for us as those things to which we respond favorably. I rely on the discretion of group leaders as to how the second *i2i* section is handled. You know your group better than I do! Some will feel comfortable sharing aloud; others may wish to use the time for silent reflection. And do remember the importance of confidentiality for any small group meeting. What is said within the group should stay within the group.

The *Day 6 Dilemma* section revolves around a difficult choice faced by characters in the novel and featured on the sixth day of each week's material. This title was also deliberately chosen to reflect the Genesis 1 account of the creation of human beings. Such choices are a fundamental part of being men and women trying to live in relationship with God.

The final section, *Living it Out*, is based upon the twelfth chapter of Romans where Paul gives some very practical advice on how to live out our lives as Christians. This chapter begins with the word 'Therefore' and follows on from the previous eleven chapters in which Paul has given a glorious exposition on no longer being slaves of the Law and sin but living in the freedom of God's Spirit. What Paul is saying is: "That was the theory. If you want to live it out in practice, here's how you do it." It will become a useful guide for us too, as we seek to relate each week's material to our everyday lives.

Direct quotations from *Les Misérables* are indicated by italics or, in the case of smaller phrases, single quotation marks. Quotations have been taken from the following English translations: Norman Denny, Penguin, 1982; Lee Fahnestock and Norman MacAfee, Signet Classic, 1987; Isabel Hapgood, 1887 – freely available through Kindle or as a download from Project Gutenberg.

Bible passages are taken from the New International Version unless otherwise indicated.

# I

# Grace

*The man opened his eyes in astonishment.*
*"Really? You knew what I was called?"*
*"Yes," replied the bishop, "you are called my brother."*

## Week I – Day I

*Read Luke 14:12-27*

We are embarking upon a journey. The journey is a historical one as it takes us through some turbulent years in the history of France. The journey is a personal one as we follow one man and his struggles with life, faith and conscience. And the journey is a timeless one as we become involved ourselves and realize that the major themes of this book are our concerns too.

The events of *Les Misérables* take place in three main locations. The book begins in Digne (1815), a town in the South of France between the Alps and Provence. Here we witness the conversion of the main character, Jean Valjean. The story then moves to Montreuil-Sur-Mer (1817-1823) in the North of France which, today, is just under an hour's drive from Calais. Finally, the bulk of the action occurs in Paris (1823-1833). Through it all, the lives of our main characters will intertwine.

The France of which Victor Hugo was writing had gone through a period of great upheaval. The French Revolution of 1789 was a political coup which ousted King Louis XVI and established a republic. This was followed by a military coup in 1799 as Napoleon Bonaparte seized control and went on, in 1804, to declare himself emperor. Under Napoleon's command, France's empire grew and grew, until an ill-fated drive into Russia in 1812 proved his downfall. In 1814, he was exiled and the monarchy was re-established under Louis XVIII. 1815 saw the brief return of Napoleon but after defeat at Waterloo it really was the end. The reigns of Louis XVIII and his successor Charles X were marked by a renewed disdain for constitutional government and matters reached a head in July 1830 with barricades and fighting on the streets of Paris. The result was a political compromise. Charles X and the Bourbon dynasty went into exile to be replaced by the 'grey banker' Louis Philippe. This restored the peace but lack of any further major constitutional reforms meant that agitation stayed close to the surface. It would return again in 1832 and form part of our story.

The early years of the nineteenth century also saw turmoil in the wider area of Western Europe.

- It was a time of political turmoil as countries continued to move from the absolutism of monarchy to more democratic systems of government.

- It was a time of military turmoil with countless wars being fought and no country being exempt.

- It was a time of economic turmoil as any prolonged period of war always is.

- It was a time of demographic turmoil as the flow from country to city, sparked by the Industrial Revolution, continued unabated.

- It was a time of climatic turmoil as Europe remained under the grip of a mini-ice age.

All of these factors had their effects within society but as always the effects were felt most strongly by those least able to cope – the poor. These are the *misérables* of the title.

One of Hugo's chief intentions was to draw attention to the plight of the poor and the systems that oppressed them. In a letter to the publisher of the Italian edition of the book he wrote:

*You are right, sir, when you tell me that Les Misérables is written for all nations. I do not know whether it will be read by all, but I wrote it for all. It is addressed to England as well as to Spain, to Italy as well as to France, to Germany as well as to Ireland, to*

*Republics which have slaves as well as to Empires which have serfs. Social problems overstep frontiers. The sores of the human race, those great sores which cover the globe, do not halt at the red or blue lines traced upon the map. In every place where man is ignorant and despairing, in every place where woman is sold for bread, wherever the child suffers for lack of the book which should instruct him and of the hearth which should warm him, the book of Les Misérables knocks at the door and says: "Open to me, I come for you."*

In 2001, George W. Bush spoke of the war against terrorism being a crusade. He very quickly discovered that certain words can be explosive. In some minds, the immediate association was with bloody medieval battles as Christians sought to wrest Jerusalem from the 'Muslim infidel'. Why then use the word in the title of this book?

Firstly, the line 'Will you join in our crusade?' comes from the closing song in the musical version of *Les Misérables* to which we shall return later.

Secondly, because the word 'crusade' returns us to the idea of a journey. As we journey through Lent, we accompany Jean Valjean and Jesus on the road to the cross.

On Ash Wednesday many Christians will be marked with a cross of ash from the burning of the previous year's palm crosses. That is actually the derivation of the word crusade. It comes from the Latin word that means 'to mark with a cross'. The medieval crusaders certainly heeded Jesus' challenge. They were prepared to pick up their crosses and lay down their lives in Jesus' name. Yet they also illustrate the pitfalls awaiting us. Jesus does not show us a destructive God who calls us to violence but an all-including God who sends us out to the vulnerable – the poor, crippled, blind and lame. How easy it is for us to be diverted from God's plan by our own agendas.

Reflect for a moment on these words from the Ash Wednesday

liturgy and the times that we are so sidetracked that we fail to see the *misérables*.

> *"We confess to you, O God, all our past unfaithfulness: the pride, hypocrisy and impatience of our lives, our self-indulgence and our exploitation of other people.*
>
> *We confess our preoccupation with worldly goods and comforts, and our envy of others.*
>
> *We confess our blindness to human need and suffering, our indifference to injustice and cruelty, our misuse and pollution of creation, and our lack of concern for the generations to come."*
>
> (© 1999 Trustees for Methodist Church Purposes)

Finally, 'crusade' in its modern usage has the sense of a campaign to make things better. As we journey, remember that God doesn't just want to change you. God wants to use you to change the world.

# Week 1 – Day 2

*Read John 3:1-17*

The book of Exodus tells the story of God forming a covenant with Israel. At the center of that relationship is obedience and the keeping of the Law. By the time of Jesus, these laws and command-ments had swelled so much with interpretations and clarifications that it would have been virtually impossible to remember the whole lot, let alone keep it. Those who tried hardest to keep the Law and to ensure that others did so were the Pharisees.

When Jesus met with the Pharisee Nicodemus, it was a meeting of old school and new school. There was, literally, a new wind of the Spirit blowing. Jesus tells Nicodemus that, if anyone wants to be part of God's Kingdom, trying to keep the Law isn't enough. That person must also undergo a radical change of heart and mind akin to being born again.

The problem with the Law is that, on its own, it cannot produce righteousness. It can only tell somebody when they have fallen short. As such, it is continually condemning. That would be OK if you took Paul's approach or that of the writer of Hebrews. Paul writes that the Law was only ever intended to be like the paedagogos, the household slave who was responsible for keeping the children of a family in check until they were suffi-ciently mature to go to school (Galatians 3). Likewise, in Hebrews 11, we are given a long list of Old Testament greats and told that they weren't saved by their adherence to the Law but by their faith.

If people aren't going to be saved by keeping the Law then how will they be saved? Jesus points the way. In the wilderness, poisonous snakes had attacked the Israelites and many had died. God commanded Moses to make a snake and to parade it at the top of a long pole. If anyone who had been bitten looked at this snake they were healed. In the same way, Jesus predicts his own death lifted high on the cross. Anyone who trusts in him will be saved to eternal life.

And then come these tremendous thoughts. God's love for us is so amazing that he will hold nothing back – not even his son – in his attempts to win us. God is truly on our side. God's love in Jesus is not a condemning force like the Law. Jesus is not there to condemn us but to save us, to bring us life. Paul takes up the theme as he writes to the early church in Rome.

*Therefore, there is now no condemnation for those who are in Christ Jesus, because through Christ Jesus the law of the Spirit of life set me free from the law of sin and death. For what the law was powerless to do in that it was weakened by the sinful nature, God did by sending his own Son in the likeness of sinful man to be a sin offering. (Romans 8:1-3 NIV1984)*

The tension between the old covenant and the new covenant, between law and grace, is one that runs through the whole of *Les Misérables*. It is represented in the book's two central characters, the reformed convict Jean Valjean and Inspector Javert, the policeman who personifies the Old Testament Law.

Javert is born in prison, the son of a convict and a fortune-teller. His career choice is motivated by the thought that his only hope of escaping from the dregs of humanity is to step outside of society as its guardian.

We are introduced to Javert as a tall figure dressed in a grey coat with cane and battered hat. He is ever vigilant with a cat's vision in the half-light. He never shows emotion and hardly ever laughs. On the few occasions that he takes leisure time, he chooses the company of a book (which he hates!). His faith in law and authority is total.

*This man was composed of two very simple and two very good sentiments, comparatively; but he rendered them almost bad, by dint of exaggerating them; respect for authority, hatred of rebellion; and in his eyes, murder, robbery, all crimes, are only forms of rebellion. He enveloped in a blind and profound faith everyone who had a function in the state, from the prime minister to the rural policeman. He covered with scorn, aversion, and disgust everyone who had once crossed the legal threshold of evil. He was absolute, and admitted no exceptions.*

He conducts his business with unwavering precision. If a law has been broken then there is a price to pay, whoever the culprit:

*He would have arrested his own father escaping from prison and denounced his mother for breaking parole, and he would have done it with a glow of conscious rectitude.*

His personal life matches his zeal for justice. He has complete integrity so that, when he thinks he has overstepped the mark with a superior, his immediate response is to offer his resignation. He never lies.

Javert is often portrayed as being on a personal quest to capture Valjean. This is incorrect and is to give him an emotional edge that is simply not there. He is totally dispassionate. When their paths cross, he is on Valjean's trail like a bloodhound. At other times, however, he is absorbed in fighting crime elsewhere.

We are offered a man who is both simple and complex. Javert is someone who should be a hero. He is missing just one thing yet that one thing is sufficient for him to be turned from hero to villain. He lacks the inner spark of love and mercy that would give him a perspective beyond the letter of the law. He is, in short, a Pharisee, blind to the deeper things of God and misinterpreting the salvation of God in others.

## Week I – Day 3

*Read Matthew 25:31-40*

*Early in the month of October, 1815, about an hour before sunset, a man who was travelling on foot entered the little town of Digne. ... It was difficult to encounter a wayfarer of more wretched appearance. He was a man of medium stature, thickset and robust, in the prime of life. He might have been forty-six or forty-eight years old. A cap with a drooping leather visor partly concealed his face, burned and tanned by sun and wind, and dripping with perspiration. His shirt of coarse yellow linen, fastened at the neck by a small silver anchor, permitted a view of his hairy breast: he had a cravat twisted into a string; trousers of blue drilling, worn and threadbare, white on one knee and torn on the other; an old grey, tattered blouse, patched on one of the elbows with a bit of green cloth sewed on with twine; a tightly packed soldier knapsack, well buckled and perfectly new, on his back; an enormous, knotty stick in his hand; iron-shod shoes on his stockingless feet; a shaved head and a long beard.*

Thus are we introduced to Jean Valjean, the central character of *Les Misérables*. His story is simple yet tragic. He is a victim with a capital V. He is born into a peasant family and, whilst young, loses both of his parents. He is brought up by his only surviving sister, an older sister. When her husband dies, Valjean reluctantly assumes the role of breadwinner for the family, earning what money he can and working until he drops. We are told, poignantly, that he has never been in love. The story gets worse:

*In pruning season he earned eighteen sous a day; then he hired out as a hay-maker, as laborer, as neat-herd on a farm, as a drudge. He did whatever he could. His sister worked also but what could she do with seven little children? It was a sad group enveloped in misery, which was being gradually annihilated. A very hard winter came. Jean had no work. The family had no bread. No bread literally. Seven children!*

*One Sunday evening, Maubert Isabeau, the baker on the Church Square at Faverolles, was preparing to go to bed, when he heard a violent blow on the grated front of his shop. He arrived in time to see an arm passed through a hole made by a blow from a fist, through the grating and the glass. The arm seized a loaf of bread and carried it off.*

The thief was Jean Valjean who is sentenced to five years' hard labor. Four times he tries to escape from prison and because of this his initial five-year sentence is extended bit by bit to nineteen years. Eventually he is released, the man we have met walking into Digne in 1815. Two decades of imprisonment have taken their toll.

*From year to year this soul had dried away slowly, but with fatal sureness. When the heart is dry, the eye is dry. On his departure from the galleys it had been nineteen years since he had shed a tear.*

Brutalized, he has withdrawn into himself and silently rages against the system that has treated him in this way. And society adds insult to injury. On Valjean's release he is captivated by the prospect of freedom but is quickly disillusioned. He has to carry special yellow papers which mark him out as an ex-convict. He does a day's work unloading bales but, when the foreman sees the papers, he refuses to pay any more than half the agreed rate. Valjean fumes. This is no less a robbery than his stealing of the loaf.

In Digne he asks for food and lodging and is refused. He asks for a glass of water and is refused. He tries to sleep in a kennel and even the dog chases him away. He feels that everyone and everything is against him.

*In that obscure and wan shadow within which he crawled, each time that he turned his neck and essayed to raise his glance, he perceived with terror, mingled with rage, a sort of frightful accumulation of things, collecting and mounting above him, beyond the range of his vision; laws, prejudices, men, and deeds, whose outlines escaped him, whose mass terrified him, and which was nothing else than that prodigious pyramid which we call civilization.*

*Betrayed,* by the English singer-songwriter Peter Hammill, is one of the gloomiest songs you will ever come across. I can't help feeling that Jean Valjean would have sympathized with its lyrics.

It speaks of setting out altruistically with plenty of hope and a faith in the goodness of humanity. This is dashed in discovering that humanity is, well, human and characterized by four base instincts – bitterness; pride; hatred and lust. Everyone, including friends, will take their opportunity to stab you in the back. This may stem from familiar roots such as revenge or spite or, more downright depressing, simply out of boredom and a lack of more interesting things to do. The bleak conclusion:

*"I don't give a damn anymore – I've only wound up betrayed. ... I've nothing left to fight for except making my passion heard – I don't believe in anything, anywhere in the world".*

How do we break through the chains of embitterment that encircle so many people? Jesus points us in the direction of selfless love. Nothing less will do. And, when we do step out of our comfort zone and reach out to others, we find that we are reaching out to Jesus.

# Week 1 – Day 4

*Read John 6:53-63*

François Melchior Charles Bienvenu de Miollis was bishop of the French town of Digne from 1805 to 1838. He was a larger than life character with a considerable reputation for charitable works and being on the side of the poor. Victor Hugo uses him as inspiration for the fictional bishop who proves the catalyst that launches Jean Valjean on a fresh journey through life. Bishop Miollis becomes Bishop Charles François Bienvenu Myriel.

In the musical version of *Les Misérables*, the bishop comes and goes in just a few lines yet in the book he fills the first hundred pages. He is described to us thus,

> *There are men who toil at extracting gold; he toiled at the extraction of pity. Universal misery was his mine. The sadness which reigned everywhere was but an excuse for unfailing kindness. Love each other; he declared this to be complete, desired nothing further, and that was the whole of his doctrine.*

He is the living embodiment of Jesus Christ who literally overflows with love and whose door is never bolted day or night.

> *As for the bishop, his thought can be found explained, or at least indicated, in the three lines which he wrote on the margin of a Bible, "This is the shade of difference: the door of the physician should never be shut, the door of the priest should always be open."*

Myriel becomes Bishop of Digne in 1806 and moves into the bishop's palace with his unmarried sister and their housekeeper. The palace is next door to the tiny hospital where twenty-six beds are cramped into its few small rooms whilst the palace can sleep sixty. To the bishop the solution is obvious. They swap.

His annual income as bishop is 15,000 francs and his distribution of this money demonstrates his commitment to those in need:

| | |
|---|---:|
| *For the little seminary* | *1500* |
| *Society of the mission* | *100* |
| *For the Lazarists of Montdidier* | *100* |
| *Seminary for foreign missions in Paris* | *200* |
| *Congregation of the Holy Spirit* | *150* |
| *Religious establishments of the Holy Land* | *100* |
| *Charitable maternity societies* | *300* |
| *Extra, for that of Arles* | *50* |
| *Work for the amelioration of prisons* | *400* |
| *Work for the relief and delivery of prisoners* | *500* |
| *To liberate fathers of families incarcerated for debt* | *1000* |
| *Addition to the salary of the poor teachers of the diocese* | *2000* |
| *Public granary of the Hautes-Alpes* | *100* |
| *For the gratuitous instruction of poor girls* | *1500* |
| *For the poor* | *6000* |
| *My personal expenses* | *1000* |
| *Total* | *15000* |

The personal expenses of 1000 francs, together with the sister's small annuity, means that the three live very simply on 1500 francs. Hoping for more income, Myriel's housekeeper reminds him that he can claim a further 3000 francs each year as a carriage allowance. The claim is duly made. The money is given to the poor and the bishop continues to ride everywhere on horseback. The one luxury that Myriel allows himself to retain is his silverware – six sets of knives and forks, a soup ladle and two candlesticks.

Neither is his ministry restricted to the relief of poverty. He is also critical of its causes:

*He was indulgent towards women and poor people, on whom the burden of human society rest. He said, "The faults of women, of children, of the feeble, the indigent, and the ignorant, are the fault of the husbands, the fathers, the masters, the strong, the rich, and the wise." He said, moreover, "Teach those who are ignorant as many things as possible; society is culpable, in that it does not afford instruction gratis; it is responsible for the night which it produces. This soul is full of shadow; sin is therein committed. The guilty one is not the person who has committed the sin, but the person who has created the shadow." It will be perceived that he had a peculiar manner of his own of judging things: I suspect that he obtained it from the Gospel.*

The bishop is an old man and his area of responsibility is a mountainous region difficult to negotiate on horseback. Neither of these factors prevents him from fulfilling his pastoral duties.

*He was at home in the peasant's hut and in the mountains. He could expound great matters in the simplest terms, and speaking all tongues could find his way to all hearts.*

On one occasion, he is advised not to travel into bandit country. His philosophy:

*"Let us never fear robbers nor murderers. Those are dangers from without, petty dangers. Let us fear ourselves. Prejudices are the real robbers; vices are the real murderers. The great dangers lie within ourselves. What matters it what threatens our head or our purse! Let us think only of that which threatens our soul."*

He makes the journey and returns with valuables previously stolen from the cathedral. His only uncertainty is whether they should be returned to the cathedral or given to the hospital.

The word disciple is the English translation of the Greek word μαθητής (mathetes) which means one who learns from another. A disciple of a master was one who learned principles from that person and put them into practice. Jesus, however, states that to be one of his followers we must take a further step. There will be no real life in us unless we make a complete identification with him. We must eat his flesh and drink his blood!

This is true discipleship and it is small wonder that people complained it was too hard! Yet, only by this can we expect to make an impact. And please note that any of us can make an impact. Too often we write ourselves off as being useless. We are too young or too old. We are untalented or uneducated. We are too timid or too impulsive. We dream up excuse after excuse but every single person with the tiniest piece of faith in their hearts is capable of moving mountains. In 1815 Bishop Myriel was seventy-five years old. Nobody would have begrudged him a quiet and peaceful retirement had he chosen it but Bishop Myriel was still living and breathing Jesus and would do so until he died. As a result, Jesus was able to use him to restore Jean Valjean – and he will use you too.

If you are looking for a cozy philosophy by which to live your life then you do not need Jesus. If you are looking to change the world in Jesus' name then read on.

# Week 1 – Day 5

*Read Luke 19:1-10*

It is time for Valjean and the bishop to meet. We left Valjean alone and dejected in the middle of Digne. There he meets a woman coming out of the cathedral who points him in the direction of the one door where he might find a welcome.

Meanwhile, in the bishop's residence, word has arrived about the 'dangerous criminal' in the town. Myriel's housekeeper is urging that they should secure the house with locks and bolts when there comes a loud knocking at the door. Unperturbed by what might lie on the other side, the bishop calls out, "Come in."

Valjean is made welcome. A meal is prepared for him and the table laid with the silverware, as it would be for an honored visitor. A bottle of wine is opened, wine reserved for guests as the bishop classes it too expensive for his own needs. And Valjean is given a bed for the night, the first proper bed he has slept in for nineteen years.

Ironically, it is the comfort of the bed that wakes him at two in the morning. Prison has transformed him into something less than human and at this point his baser instincts take over. He has already reckoned the value of the silver cutlery as being twice what he earned from two decades in prison and he feels that society owes him with the church being a central prop of all that has rejected him. Consequently, he makes off with the cutlery. He does not get far and two policemen bring him back to the bishop's house:

*A singular and violent group made its appearance on the threshold. Three men were holding a fourth man by the collar. The three men were gendarmes; the other was Jean Valjean. ... "Ah! Here you are!" he exclaimed, looking at Jean Valjean. "I am glad to see you. Well, but how is this? I gave you the candlesticks too, which are of* silver like the rest, and for which you can certainly get two hundred francs. Why did you not carry them away with your forks and spoons?" Jean Valjean opened his eyes wide, and stared at the venerable bishop with an expression which no human tongue can render any account of.

"Monseigneur," said the brigadier of gendarmes, "so what this man said is true, then? We came across him. He was walking like a man who is running away. We stopped him to look into the matter. He had this silver ..."

"And he told you," interposed the bishop with a smile, "that it had been given to him by a kind old fellow of a priest with whom he had passed the night? I see how the matter stands. And you have brought him back here? It is a mistake."

"In that case," replied the brigadier, "we can let him go?"

"Certainly," replied the bishop. The gendarmes released Jean Valjean, who recoiled.

"Is it true that I am to be released?" he said, in an almost inarticulate voice, and as though he were talking in his sleep.

"Yes, you're released; do you not understand?" said one of the gendarmes.

"My friend," resumed the bishop, "before you go, here are your candlesticks. Take them."

He stepped to the chimney-piece, took the two silver candlesticks, and brought them to Jean Valjean. The two women looked on without uttering a word, without a gesture, without a look which could disconcert the bishop. Jean Valjean was trembling in every limb. He took the two candlesticks mechanically, and with a bewildered air.

"Now," said the bishop, "go in peace. By the way, when you return, my friend, it is not necessary to pass through the garden. You can always enter and depart through the street door. It is never fastened with anything but a latch, either by day or by night."

Then, turning to the gendarmes: "You may retire, gentlemen." The gendarmes retired. Jean Valjean was like a man on the point *of fainting.*

*The bishop drew near to him, and said in a low voice: "Do not forget, never forget, that you have promised to use this money in becoming an honest man."*

*Jean Valjean, who had no recollection of ever having promised anything, remained speechless. The bishop had emphasized the words when he uttered them. He resumed with solemnity: "Jean Valjean, my brother, you no longer belong to evil, but to good. It is your soul that I buy from you; I withdraw it from black thoughts and the spirit of perdition, and I give it to God."*

Grace is a difficult word to define but here we have it expressed perfectly. Mercy is not being treated as one deserves when one has done wrong. Had the bishop refused to press charges against Valjean it would have been merciful. Grace goes beyond that. Mercy wipes out a negative. Grace adds a positive. If mercy is not being punished as we deserve then grace is being given something we don't deserve. Grace is two candlesticks taken from a mantelpiece and given to a thief.

In Jesus' time to eat and drink with somebody was a sign that you had nothing against that person. That was one of the reasons why the Pharisees got upset when Jesus ate with 'sinners' because it looked as though he was approving of their actions. Zaccheus was a man who, like Valjean, was reviled by polite society. Why? Because he was a tax collector and tax collectors collaborated with the Roman occupiers, as well as having a notorious reputation for over-charging! Very few people would have accepted an invitation to one of his dinner parties and even fewer would have invited him to one of theirs. It was a life that would have left him well-hardened.

How do you warm the heart of a hard person? Not by giving them what they deserve but by giving them more than they deserve. That is grace. That was Jesus.

## Week I – Day 6

*Read Matthew 4:12-17*

The bishop had given Valjean the two silver candlesticks with the words that his soul was now bought for God but on their own those words have no meaning. If they did there would be no need for any of us to be praying for non-Christian family or friends. Instead, we could simply bring them into God's Kingdom by our own actions. What we do may have a profound impact in the lives of other people but each of those people has to decide for themselves how they will respond and what future direction their lives will take.

As Jesus begins his ministry, he appropriates the words of the prophet Isaiah. Light is dawning where there had been only darkness and shadows. So it is with Valjean. The bishop's kindness – the grace that had been shown to him – was beginning to penetrate the darkness of his mind.

What is the one further thing needed in order to respond to that light? Repent, says Jesus, because the Kingdom of Heaven is near. The Greek word used here is the word μετανοέω (metanoeo). It means, literally, to change one's mind. Where once we did the wrong thing, now we see the error of our ways and choose to do the right thing. It has been said that in Jesus' time the word would have been perfectly understood on a military parade ground. If the word μετανοέω were barked out, any soldier in earshot would perform a 180-degree turn and begin marching in the opposite direction. That too is exactly what the word means spiritually. It is to stop marching away from God and to begin running into his arms.

It is hard to think of the word repent without adding 'of your sins' but that is to undersell it. The emphasis is just as much, if not more, on what we are turning to rather than what we are turning from. We don't come to God because we have turned our back on sin. We turn our back on sin because we have chosen to turn to God.

Having left the bishop, Valjean is in turmoil.

*He was indistinctly conscious that the pardon of this priest was the greatest assault and the most formidable attack which had moved him yet; that his obduracy was finally settled if he resisted this clemency; that if he yielded, he should be obliged to renounce that hatred with which the actions of other men had filled his soul through so many years, and which pleased him ...*

So troubled is he that he enters a near trance-like state and when a small boy's coin rolls under his foot he instinctively covers it with his foot and seems not to notice the boy's cries. It is one further offence and one that is to have devastating consequences. As an ex-convict, any fresh offence will throw him back into prison. This is that offence. From now on, the threat of reincarceration will follow Valjean through the remainder of the book.

But when he finally realizes what he has done, it proves the key that is needed to unlock Valjean's spiritual life.

*First of all, even before examining himself and reflecting, all bewildered, like one who seeks to save himself, he tried to find the child in order to return his money to him; then, when he recognized the fact that this was impossible, he halted in despair.*

*At the moment when he exclaimed "I am a wretch!" he had just perceived what he was, and he was already separated from himself to such a degree, that he seemed to himself to be no longer anything more than a phantom, and as if he had, there before him in flesh and blood, the hideous galley-convict, Jean Valjean, cudgel in hand, his blouse on his hips, his knapsack filled with stolen objects on his back, with his resolute and gloomy visage, with his thoughts filled with abominable projects.*

*... Thus he contemplated himself, so to speak, face to face, and at*

*the same time, athwart this hallucination, he perceived in a myste-*
*rious depth a sort of light which he at first took for a torch. On*
*scrutinizing this light which appeared to his conscience with more*
*attention, he recognized the fact that it possessed a human form and*
*that this torch was the bishop.*

*His conscience weighed in turn these two men thus placed before*
*it; the bishop and Jean Valjean. Nothing less than the first was*
*required to soften the second. By one of those singular effects, which*
*are peculiar to this sort of ecstasies, in proportion as his revery*
*continued, as the bishop grew great and resplendent in his eyes, so*
*did Jean Valjean grow less and vanish. After a certain time he was*
*no longer anything more than a shade. All at once he disappeared.*
*The bishop alone remained; he filled the whole soul of this wretched*
*man with a magnificent radiance.*

*Jean Valjean wept for a long time. He wept burning tears, he*
*sobbed with more weakness than a woman, with more fright than a*
*child. As he wept, daylight penetrated more and more clearly into*
*his soul; an extraordinary light; a light at once ravishing and*
*terrible. His past life, his first fault, his long expiation, his external*
*brutishness, his internal hardness, his dismissal to liberty, rejoicing*
*in manifold plans of vengeance, what had happened to him at the*
*bishop's, the last thing that he had done, that theft of forty sous from*
*a child, a crime all the more cowardly, and all the more monstrous*
*since it had come after the bishop's pardon; all this recurred to his*
*mind and appeared clearly to him, but with a clearness which he had*
*never hitherto witnessed. He examined his life, and it seemed*
*horrible to him; his soul, and it seemed frightful to him. In the*
*meantime a gentle light rested over this life and this soul. It seemed*
*to him that he beheld Satan by the light of Paradise.*

*How many hours did he weep thus? What did he do after he had*
*wept? Whither did he go! No one ever knew. The only thing which*
*seems to be authenticated is that that same night the carrier who*
*served Grenoble at that time, and who arrived at Digne about three*
*o'clock in the morning, saw, as he traversed the street in which the*

*bishop's residence was situated, a man in the attitude of prayer, kneeling on the pavement in the shadow, in front of the door of Monseigneur Bienvenu.*

# Week I – Day 7

Questions for personal reflection or group discussion

Keyword for the week: Grace

## Setting the scene
Watch the DVD (14 minutes)
Start: Scene 1, the beginning of the movie
Finish: Valjean tears up his papers and throws the pieces into the air (13:45)

## i 2 i
*Issues to explore*
What stood out for you from this week's readings or movie clip?
Was there anything you didn't understand?
*Irritants*
Was there anything in the material with which you disagreed?

## The Day 6 Dilemma
The struggle that comes from being a person created in the image of God

The bishop's actions provoked a great struggle in Valjean out of which came faith.
What was it that prompted Valjean to change?
What was pulling him in the opposite direction?
How might you have reacted in his situation?

## Living it out

*Therefore, I urge you, brothers and sisters, in view of God's mercy, to offer your bodies as a living sacrifice, holy and pleasing to God — this is your true and proper worship. Do not conform to the pattern of this world, but be transformed by the renewing of your mind. Then you will be able to test and approve what God's will is—his good, pleasing and perfect will. (Romans 12:1-2)*

How would you define the following phrases?

'Offer your bodies as a living sacrifice';

'The pattern of this world';

'The renewing of your mind'.

Why do you think we cannot properly know God's will without undergoing a transformation of our mind?

What do you think are the main things that stop a person from becoming a Christian?

How would you define grace? How can we live our lives so that God's grace shines through us as it did the bishop?

**i 2 i**

*Insights*

What insights have you gained from this week's material?

*Implementation*

Did you resolve to change anything in your life? What steps do you need to take to achieve this?

# 2

# Responsibility

*It is a terrible thing to be happy! How pleased we are with it!*
*How all-sufficient we think it!*
*How, being in possession of the false aim of life, happiness,*
*we forget the true aim, duty!*

## Week 2 – Day 1

*Read Matthew 25:14-30*

What happens to Jean Valjean after he leaves Digne? He sells the bishop's silverware, keeping just the two candlesticks as a reminder. He works his way across France until eventually in 1817 he comes to the town of Montreuil-Sur-Mer. By now he has assumed a fresh identity. He has become Monsieur Madeleine.

Valjean becomes wealthy and makes the town wealthy with him.

*He was a stranger in the Department. Of his origin, nothing was known; of the beginning of his career, very little. It was rumored that he had come to town with very little money, a few hundred francs at the most. It was from this slender capital, enlisted in the service of an ingenious idea, developed by method and thought, that he had drawn his own fortune, and the fortune of the whole countryside.*

This 'ingenious idea' has led to a revolution in the local manufacturing industry. Do not miss the irony and God's sense of humor. He has enabled the man with the fake identity to make his fortune manufacturing – fake jewelry! Within two years he is able to build a new factory with two large workshops, one for men and one for women, in order that 'they might remain virtuous'. Those in need only have to apply in order to be given a job and a living wage. All that was required was: of the men, good will; of the women, pure morals; and, of all, integrity. It wasn't just the factory workers who benefited but, we are told, due to the trickle-down effect, there was not one family in the town that did not benefit in some way or other.

Valjean has only two aims in life. One is to keep his true identity hidden. The other is, in the most anonymous way possible, to do all the good that he can and thereby 'find his way back to God'. As we shall see, these two goals could sometimes come into conflict and when they did, the latter always took priority over the former.

By 1820 Valjean has a total of 635,000 francs deposited with his bankers. When you have those amounts of money passing through your hands it's hard to stay anonymous. He ploughs a million francs into the public services of the town. He delights in giving money to the poor. He is noted in high places and the King seeks to appoint him as the town's mayor. Valjean refuses. Likewise he turns down the honor of the Grand Cross when it is offered to him. Finally, spurred on by public opinion, the King again tries to appoint him as mayor.

*It was said that what had induced him to change his mind were the words shouted at him almost angrily by an old woman standing in her doorway – 'A good mayor is a useful person. How can you hold back when you have the chance to do good?'*

Matthew and Luke both give us the parable of the talents but in slightly different forms. The key elements are, however, the same. Both stories involve a man going away for a long period and giving his servants the responsibility of managing his money wisely. The sums in Luke are smaller but in Matthew these amounts, reckoned in talents, are fabulous sums of money. Each person is given an amount proportional to their ability. There is little doubt that the early Christians interpreted this parable as applying to themselves and what we do with the gifts that have been given to us as we wait for the second coming of Jesus.

The first servant has doubled his five talents to ten. The second has doubled his two to four. Both servants are praised and rewarded with greater responsibility. I always find it reassuring to remember that it is actually the second servant who has done better despite returning the smaller amount. If you don't believe me, do the math. Each was given money according to their ability. That meant that the first servant was expected to outperform the second. In the end they both achieved the same increase – 100 percent – thereby meaning that the second servant actually exceeded expectations. It is a comforting thought when we compare our abilities unfavorably with other people. God does not judge on who seems the best but on what we have done with what we have been given.

The third servant has done nothing with his one talent. He is criticized and his money is given to the first servant. I always had a problem with that part. Why should the one with ten talents be given more? Until I realized that Jesus is not talking about personal wealth – all the money still belongs to the master – but responsibility for the money. Jesus is saying that if God can trust us with responsibility then more will come our way. If God cannot trust us then he will not entrust anything to us. It's just like the years I spent training to be an accountant. We started with small tasks, took exams, learned on the job and, as we progressed and showed ourselves capable, more and more responsibility came our way. Fail and you did not complete your training.

Jean Valjean had made a fresh start. Under God's guidance he had made full use of his entrepreneurial skills and God had entrusted more and more to him, right up to governing the town (which is the reward given to faithful servants in Luke's version of the parable). All of us as Christians have talents and as you use them under God's direction then he will increase your responsibility. Some of us, like Valjean, will have God-given business skills. Don't hide them. Don't think of business as a dirty word. The business arena is in just as much need of Christian input as any other. Remember the words shouted from the doorway. How can you hold back when God gives you the chance to do good? Instead, resolve now to read up on some of the great Christian philanthropists of the past and let God inspire you by their example.

## Week 2 – Day 2

*Read John 15:1-17*

As we have observed, Valjean's rise is meteoric. Within five years of arriving in Montreuil-Sur-Mer he has amassed a personal fortune, transformed the town and become its mayor. Best of all, his past life appears to be behind him.

The impression he gives to the townspeople is of quiet paternalism. He is grey-haired with 'the tanned complexion of a working man and the thoughtful countenance of a philosopher'. He possesses prodigious strength and this is often put to good use if someone needs a helping hand. His agricultural background also comes in handy as he passes on tips for country living. Children love him because he always carries a pocketful of loose change and because his years in prison have taught him how to make fascinating toys from simple objects. The poor love him because 'they owe him everything'. He has great diplomatic skills:

> *People came from twenty miles around to consult Monsieur Madeleine. He resolved disputes, prevented lawsuits, reconciled enemies. Every man trusted him to judge fairly, as though his guiding spirit were a book of natural law.*

In short, he has created a little utopia on Earth in which virtually everyone is devoted to him. Yet he never seems to be particularly joyful. He is described as a friendly but sad figure, keeping himself to himself as much as possible.

> *He spoke to but few people. He avoided polite attentions; he escaped quickly; he smiled to relieve himself of the necessity of talking; he gave, in order to get rid of the necessity for smiling. The women said of him, "What a good-natured bear!" His pleasure consisted in*

*strolling in the fields. He always took his meals alone, with an open*
*book before him, which he read. He had a well-selected little library.*
*He loved books; books are cold but safe friends.*

In 1821, the newspapers reported the death of Bishop Bienvenu of
Digne. At the end of his life he had become blind but with his
sister by his side bore this with the same happy serenity with
which he faced the rest of life. Victor Hugo, in his role as narrator,
observes that blindness is transformed with a loving companion
by your side:

*The supreme happiness of life consists in the conviction that one is*
*loved; loved for one's own sake – let us say rather, loved in spite of*
*one's self; this conviction the blind man possesses. To be served in*
*distress is to be caressed. Does he lack anything? No. One does not*
*lose the sight when one has love. And what love! A love wholly*
*constituted of virtue! There is no blindness where there is certainty.*
*Soul seeks soul, gropingly, and finds it.*

There is still a striking distinction between the bishop and
Valjean. One is blind but content because of the assurance of love
in his life. The other is sighted (in both worldly and heavenly
terms) but joyless.

What was Valjean's problem? Look closely at today's reading
and you will see. I have no doubt that his was a genuine
conversion. The bishop's actions had forced him into personal
reflection and he was genuinely remorseful for his previous
behavior. He had resolved to lead a renewed life and had entered
into a living relationship with God. He had taken to heart the
command to love and his whole life was spent in putting this into
practice. He was undoubtedly part of the vine and his fruit-
fulness bears witness to that fact.

What Valjean lacked, however, was a personal experience of
love. When Jesus commanded his disciples to love it was out of

personal relationship. As the Father loved Jesus so Jesus loved his disciples and, as they remained in his love, they were to love each other in turn. Through this, he said, they would find ultimate joy. In such a relationship there was no way the disciples could be called servants of Jesus. Instead he called them and calls us – friends. Valjean was still a servant. He loved because he knew that was what Jesus wanted him to do. He did it willingly and sacrificially but had never been opened up to the depths of love himself.

The great evangelist, John Wesley, had the same problem. As a young man he adopted the faith of his parents. Whilst at Oxford University he started a little group of students with his brother Charles. The group met to read the Bible and other devotional works and to pray. They regularly attended communion together and performed charitable works in the town and its hospital and prison. There was no doubting their rigorous zeal for God which earned them various nicknames including the Holy Club and the Methodists. In 1735, both John and Charles went to America as missionaries in what seemed a natural progression from their life in Oxford. It was not what they had expected. The stresses and disappointments they experienced in America brought a realization to the surface. They had met with other Christians who had a quiet, joyful assurance in their hearts but they knew it was lacking in their own.

Both John and Charles went through what they described as conversion experiences within a few days of each other in 1738. We might more properly call it their evangelical conversion, as I do not believe their relationship with God was in question. What they did experience was an assurance of salvation that left them in no doubt about their acceptance by a loving God and which filled their lives with a peace and joy that meant their lives would never be the same again.

So many of us find ourselves alongside Valjean and the

Wesleys, particularly in the early days of faith. We know that we are Christians but our relationship with God feels more like that of a servant than a lover. If this is you, take the words of Jesus to heart. He does not call you servant but friend. He loves you with the unconditional love of the Father. He is waiting to fill you with his joy in all its fullness. All you have to do is accept.

# Week 2 – Day 3

*Read Matthew 22:34-40*

*Blachevelle loved Favourite, so named because she had been in England; Listolier adored Dahlia, who had taken for her nickname the name of a flower; Fameuil idolized Zephine, an abridgment of Josephine; Tholomyes had Fantine, called the Blonde, because of her beautiful, sunny hair.*

Felix Tholomyes is a thirty-year-old balding Parisian student who writes plays and (indifferent) verse and has a significant income. He is also the natural leader of this little group. To describe them as boyfriends and girlfriends would be not quite accurate. The girls are, in the French way, more like kept mistresses. For the boys these are passing affairs. The girls have had lovers before and will almost certainly have them again. Hugo does not condemn them for this. He understands that prettiness is a bankable asset for a poor working class girl. When a young man comes calling, they cannot afford to ignore an opportunity, even though they know in their heart of hearts that it is going nowhere.

The one exception is Fantine. She is the baby of the group and this is her 'first illusion'. It will also be her last. Everyone else may know the score but Fantine is in love and she is deadly serious. She has given herself to Tholomyes as a wife to a husband.

Fantine has no clue who her parents are and no idea of her roots. She was found as a young girl running barefoot in the streets and the name she bears came from the passer-by who found her. At the age of ten she had gone into service with a local farming family and, at fifteen, had left to seek her fortune in Paris. Here she had found work and grown into a beautiful young woman whose most striking features were her hair and her teeth.

*Fantine was beautiful, without being too conscious of it. Those rare dreamers, mysterious priests of the beautiful who silently confront everything with perfection, would have caught a glimpse in this little working-woman, through the transparency of her Parisian grace, of the ancient sacred euphony. This daughter of the shadows was thoroughbred. She was beautiful in the two ways – style and rhythm. Style is the form of the ideal; rhythm is its movement.*

For months the girls have been asking for a big surprise so, at the suggestion of Tholomyes, the boys hatch a plan. The girls are invited to a day out in the countryside. Hardly able to contain their excitement they rise at five in the morning and embark on a series of adventures. At lunch, the boys disappear to prepare their surprise. The girls wait in anticipation until finally the waiter brings them a sealed envelope. Inside is a letter, which reads:

*"THIS IS THE SURPRISE."*
*"OUR BELOVED:*
*"You must know that we have parents. Parents – you do not know much about such things. They are called fathers and mothers by the civil code, which is puerile and honest. Now, these parents groan, these old folks implore us, these good men and these good women call us prodigal sons; they desire our return, and offer to kill calves for us.*
*Being virtuous, we obey them. At the hour when you read this, five fiery horses will be bearing us to our papas and mammas. ... We return to society, to duty, to respectability, at full trot, at the rate of three leagues an hour. It is necessary for the good of the country that we should be, like the rest of the world, prefects, fathers of families, rural police, and councilors of state. Venerate us. We are sacrificing ourselves. Mourn for us in haste, and replace us with speed. If this – letter lacerates you, do the same by it. Adieu. For the space of nearly two years we have made you happy. Do not bear us ill-will."*

Three of the four girls laugh heartily, appreciating a good joke. The fourth joins in the laughter but when she gets home bursts into tears. Fantine is twenty-one, alone, and she and Tholomyes have a child.

Fantine pays – she cannot write and can barely read – to have three letters written to Tholomyes. He never replies. Hugo adds one final postscript:

> *We shall have no further occasion to speak of M. Felix Tholomyes. Let us confine ourselves to saying, that, twenty years later, under King Louis Philippe, he was a great provincial lawyer, wealthy and influential, a wise elector, and a very severe juryman; he was still a man of pleasure.*

If Jean Valjean was the epitome of responsibility then Felix Tholomyes is the epitome of irresponsibility. It is scarcely credible that a man could walk out of a situation like that without any thought of supporting a woman who is totally dependent on him and a young girl who is his daughter. And yet it happens all too often in our age too.

A wider question though. How do we ensure that our actions do not hurt others either directly or accidentally? We do it by keeping one eye on God and one on the people around us.

For a ship to know its position, anywhere in the world, it needs two bearings – latitude and longitude. That is true of the spiritual life as well. Jesus was asked which he considered to be the greatest of the commandments and he gave two in reply – 'Love the Lord your God with all your heart and with all your soul and with all your mind' and 'Love your neighbor as yourself'. These are your bearings. Follow these two commandments, Jesus said, and you will satisfy all the demands of the Old Testament scriptures whose chief purpose was to enable people to live together as God's chosen people with mutual trust, faithfulness and the fulfilling of obligations.

It is easy to rail at Tholomyes but how seriously do you take the effect of your actions on other people? God does not call us to be forever bound by our actions but he does call us to take responsibility for them.

# Week 2 – Day 4

*Read John 4:1-14*

Fantine is abandoned in Paris with a small daughter. She has no family to look to for support. The three other girls drift away as soon as the boys have left. There is nothing that binds them together. It would be easy in such circumstances to withdraw into self-pity but Fantine is made of sterner stuff. That she doesn't succeed is certainly not down to her lack of resolve.

Fantine stays on in Paris for ten months. She had given up her previous employment during her relationship with Tholomyes and now finds that there is no work available. She lives as frugally as possible, dressing in the plainest clothes, cutting out all luxuries and devoting everything to her daughter who is now two years old. The daughter's name is Euphrasie, although she is known by the pet name that her mother has given her – Cosette. Such is Fantine's devotion that Cosette is still dressed in silks and laces and has been breast-fed despite this weakening her mother's chest.

Eventually, Fantine decides to return to her hometown:

> *She was vaguely conscious that she was on the verge of falling into distress, and of gliding into a worse state. Courage was necessary; she possessed it, and held herself firm. The idea of returning to her native town of Montreuil-Sur-Mer occurred to her. There, someone might possibly know her and give her work; yes, but it would be necessary to conceal her fault. In a confused way she perceived the necessity of a separation which would be more painful than the first one. Her heart contracted, but she took her resolution. Fantine, as we shall see, had the fierce bravery of life.*

Fantine and Cosette begin their journey by taking a coach to Montfermeil, just outside of Paris. There, in front of an inn, are two little girls playing happily together. Their mother is singing sweetly beside them. Fantine sees this as a sign from Heaven and asks the innkeeper's wife whether they would take Cosette into their family until such time as Fantine can afford to have her with her. An arrangement is struck and Fantine goes on to Montreuil-Sur-Mer where she finds work in Valjean's newly opened factory.

Fantine must be applauded for trying to make the best of a terrible situation. She acts responsibly. She stays as long as she dares in Paris and then takes the painful decision to uproot and move to the place where economically she may have the best chance of providing for herself and Cosette. She has become an economic migrant.

What is an economic migrant? It is somebody who takes a decision like Fantine that economically their life would be better if they moved to another place. Sometimes that will mean transplanting an entire family. Sometimes it will mean a breadwinner moving and sending money home. And if that decision is taken responsibly, as was Fantine's, surely we should be applauding them as we applauded Fantine.

When Jesus stopped to talk with a woman at a well in Samaria it was a remarkable conversation. The conversation was remarkable for its content but it was also remarkable that the conversation took place at all.

Firstly, it is probable that the woman was of a dubious moral standing, a fact of which Jesus was fully aware. She had had five husbands and was living with a man who wasn't her husband. She was fetching water at noon, at the hottest part of the day, and it has been suggested that this was to avoid the other women who might criticize her. No upright Jewish man would engage such a woman in conversation, especially not alone.

Furthermore, many upright Jewish men wouldn't have even been traveling that way but would have lengthened their journey to go around Samaria. The enmity between Jews and Samaritans was long-standing. It went back centuries to the overthrow of the

Northern kingdom of Israel by the Assyrians (2 Kings 17). The Assyrian king deported most of the Israelites and repopulated Samaria with people from other parts of the Assyrian empire. Over time their religious practices diverged from those of the Jews. The prejudice in Israel against the Samaritans was therefore based upon two factors. In part it was a doctrinal clash as evidenced by Jesus' conversation with the woman. At heart, however, was a more sinister element that plagues all peoples in all places at all times. The Samaritans were hated because they were different. They were not true Jews.

It is remarkable, then, that Jesus stops to talk with this woman and breaks through multiple barriers of prejudice but he does more than that. Grace doesn't just accept, it provides. Jesus shares his treasure with her – the promise of eternal life.

Today we live in a world of economic migration on a global scale. People come to a foreign country seeking to better themselves or just to survive and so often they are vilified. Any politician knows that the quickest way to get easy votes is to jump on an anti-immigration bandwagon. Any newspaper editor knows that an anti-immigration campaign will provoke interest and sell papers. This is because most people exhibit the same xenophobia that the Jews of Jesus' day showed to the Samaritans. We don't like people who are different and we don't see why we should have to share our treasures with them.

What is God's take on economic migration? Other than placing Israel in the Promised Land, I don't find God creating national boundaries anywhere in my Bible but I do find him urging me to help my brothers and sisters in need, particularly when they are doing all that they can do to support themselves. Who am I to deny a share of my treasure to somebody else just because they come from a different place to me?

There is one final ironic twist to the story. The conversation takes place at Jacob's well, a name guaranteed to remind the people of the Patriarch and his sons. They would have been reminded of Joseph, his tribulations, his eventual success in Egypt and how he was able to help his family resettle in time of famine. Or, put another way, it would have reminded them that Jacob was one of the world's first economic migrants.

# Week 2 – Day 5

*Read Matthew 7:15–20*

Cosette is left with the Thenardiers, the innkeepers of Montfermeil. Far from being sweet paragons of virtue, these will turn out to be mean and dangerous. Fantine's sign from Heaven is badly misread.

What more can be said about the Thenardiers?

*They were of those dwarfed natures which, if a dull fire chances to warm them up, easily become monstrous. There was in the woman a substratum of the brute, and in the man the material for a blackguard. Both were susceptible, in the highest degree, of the sort of hideous progress which is accomplished in the direction of evil. There exist crab-like souls which are continually retreating towards the darkness, retrograding in life rather than advancing, employing experience to augment their deformity, growing incessantly worse, and becoming more and more impregnated with an ever-augmenting blackness. This man and woman possessed such souls.*

Thenardier claims to have fought at Waterloo. The inn's sign (which he had painted – badly) depicts the story that he loves to tell to customers. It shows him on the battlefield bearing another soldier on his back. The soldier he is rescuing wears the uniform of a general. Underneath is written, "The Sergeant of Waterloo".

Thenardier is small, bony, sallow-faced and puny. He is cunning, shrewd, a smooth talker, a ruffian with a gloss of education and completely hypocritical. He smiles constantly 'as a matter of precaution'. He is capable of fraud, blackmail, robbery, kidnapping and even murder. He also has a keen interest in servant girls, which is why his wife no longer keeps any! Later in the story he will be sentenced to death (in his absence). At the end of the book he will depart for a new life in

America to make his fortune in slave trading.

Madame Thenardier is a tall, red-haired and broad-shouldered woman. She is physically intimidating with a single tooth left in her mouth. She is violent and when she speaks, everything trembles. She 'swore splendidly; she boasted of being able to crack a nut with one blow of her fist'. She resembles 'those colossal wild women, who contort themselves at fairs with paving stones hanging from their hair' and could have found alternative employment at the fair as the bearded lady. At the time of her meeting with Fantine she is glued to romantic fiction. One result of this is the names given to her two girls – Eponine and Azelma. Another is her adopting 'an attitude of romantic subservience' towards her husband. Later, when reading fads change, she will become 'nothing but a coarse, vicious woman, who had dabbled in stupid romances'. There are to be three further additions to the family, all boys.

The physical descriptions might tempt you to think that Madame Thenardier is the dominant character but don't be misled. Thenardier is very much the brains of the outfit.

*This woman was a formidable creature who loved no one except her children, and who did not fear anyone except her husband. She was a mother because she was a woman. But her maternity stopped short with her daughters, and, as we shall see, did not extend to boys. The man had but one thought – how to enrich himself.*

Jesus, as he taught his disciples, warned them to watch out for wolves dressed in sheep's clothing. These would be highly credible people who would present themselves as godly but in reality would be working to their own (or worse) agenda. Instead of leading people towards God they will lead them in the opposite direction. They will be completely plausible on the surface but their actions will have a destructive effect upon the flock, hence the imagery of wolves and sheep.

These people are not confined solely to Jesus' time. They are in every time, in every place and in every church. I have seen people who achieved positions of significant leadership within the church who have been nothing but a spiritual sham. I have seen self-proclaimed prophets claiming great spiritual maturity and revelation, who have been doing nothing more than marching to the sound of their own drum and asking everyone else to fall into line behind them. I have seen marriages broken up because I wanted to believe the best of people and wasn't sufficiently tuned in to the predatory behavior that was really going on.

When so much within the Christian community relies upon trust and goodwill, how then do we ensure that we are not duped as Fantine was?

- Remember that discernment is one of the gifts of the Holy Spirit and that there is nothing wrong with healthy suspicion. Remember that Jesus prayed that his disciples would be as innocent as doves but as shrewd as snakes.

- Be aware of the motivations of your heart. This is a subject we shall return to later. Sometimes we are blind to the reality of a situation because we want to believe the best of people. Fantine bought into a picture of idyllic family life because she desperately wanted a home like that in which to leave Cosette. Never let desperation disarm discernment.

- Listen to the advice that Jesus gives in this passage. You will be able to judge people correctly, he says, by their fruit. No bad tree can produce good fruit and vice versa. If God is at work within a person then genuinely good and constructive things will result from it. Is this person loving? Are they joyful? Are they kind? Are they faithful?

Are they patient? Do they display goodness, gentleness and self-control? Those of us at the charismatic end of the fold are particularly susceptible and may have been in Jesus' mind when he uttered these words. Don't just rejoice in signs and wonders. Look for the fruit.

Fantine didn't have the luxury of time in which to put the Thenardiers to the test nor the ability to discern. The prompting she attributed to Heaven was more likely to have come from Hell. Had Fantine realized this, the story might have been entirely different.

## Week 2 – Day 6

*Read Luke 10:25-37*

You may have wondered how Valjean was able to establish himself in Montreuil-Sur-Mer without anyone checking his papers. It was due to the fact that his arrival in the town had coincided with a fire in the town hall, in which the two children of the police inspector had been trapped. Valjean had rescued them and in the excitement (or perhaps due to the father's gratitude?) his papers were never checked. Subsequently, Javert has been appointed to the role.

Javert is one of the few people in the town to have negative feelings about Valjean in his new identity as Madeleine. He is an observer par excellence with a radar instinct for anything out of place. He scrutinizes Valjean at every opportunity, convinced that they have met before. They have, as Javert's previous experience included working in prisons in the South of France.

Fauchelevent is another who dislikes Valjean but for different reasons. He was working as a law-scrivener when Valjean first came to the town. His business was going downhill then and subsequently went bust. He watched the rise and rise of Madeleine and resented the fact that this man, no more than a day laborer, was succeeding whilst he, a professional, was failing. Jealousy took over and since then he has acted against Valjean whenever he can.

These three men come together to provide Valjean with his first great dilemma as a Christian. When Fauchelevent's business went bankrupt he was left with only a horse and cart and so began a new career as a carrier. One day, Valjean comes upon a crowd of people. Coming to the front he discovers that Fauchelevent's horse has fallen, breaking both back legs. The cart has fallen on Fauchelevent and is slowly crushing him.

M. Madeleine arrived. People stood aside respectfully. "Help!" cried
old Fauchelevent. "Who will be good and save the old man?" M.
Madeleine turned towards those present: "Is there a jack-screw to be
had?"

"One has been sent for," answered the peasant.

"How long will it take to get it?"

"They have gone for the nearest, to Flachot's place, where there
is a farrier; but it makes no difference; it will take a good quarter of
an hour."

"A quarter of an hour!" exclaimed Madeleine.

It had rained on the preceding night; the soil was soaked. The cart
was sinking deeper into the earth every moment, and crushing the
old carter's breast more and more.

It was evident that his ribs would be broken in five minutes more.

"It is impossible to wait another quarter of an hour," said
Madeleine to the peasants, who were staring at him. "We must!"

"But it will be too late then! Don't you see that the cart is
sinking?"

"Well!"

"Listen," resumed Madeleine; "there is still room enough under
the cart to allow a man to crawl beneath it and raise it with his back.
Only half a minute, and the poor man can be taken out. Is there any
one here who has stout loins and heart? There are five louis d'or to
be earned!" Not a man in the group stirred.

"Ten louis," said Madeleine.

The persons present dropped their eyes. One of them muttered:
"A man would need to be devilish strong. And then he runs the risk
of getting crushed!"

"Come," began Madeleine again, "twenty louis." The same
silence.

"It is not the will which is lacking," said a voice. M. Madeleine
turned round, and recognized Javert. He had not noticed him on his
arrival.

Javert went on: "It is strength. One would have to be a terrible *man to do such a thing as lift a cart like that on his back."*

*Then, gazing fixedly at M. Madeleine, he went on, emphasizing every word that he uttered: "Monsieur Madeleine, I have never known but one man capable of doing what you ask."*

*Madeleine shuddered.*

*Javert added, with an air of indifference, but without removing his eyes from Madeleine: "He was a convict."*

*"Ah!" said Madeleine.*

*"In the galleys at Toulon."*

*Madeleine turned pale.*

*Meanwhile, the cart continued to sink slowly. Father Fauchelevent rattled in the throat, and shrieked: "I am strangling! My ribs are breaking! A screw! Something! Ah!"*

*Madeleine glanced about him. "Is there, then, no one who wishes to earn twenty louis and save the life of this poor old man?"*

*No one stirred. Javert resumed: "I have never known but one man who could take the place of a screw and he was that convict."*

*"Ah! It is crushing me!" cried the old man.*

It is a terrible dilemma to face. Doing nothing means that you will be safe but risks the life of another human being lying in agony in front of you. Doing good means that a life will be saved but you risk bad things happening to you. The temptation must also be there to say that this is a man who wishes you nothing but evil. You don't owe him anything. What would you do?

That in a nutshell was the dilemma facing the three characters on the road between Jericho and Jerusalem. Each of them came upon the prostrate and naked body of a man attacked by robbers. We can speculate as to reasons why the priest and Levite chose not to stop but at the forefront of all three of those minds would have been these simple facts. This is a lonely road. This is bandit country. This might be an ambush. What would you do?

Jesus said that it was only the Samaritan who had the guts and the charity to rise above fear, prejudice and his own self-interest to help the man. And Jesus calls you to go and do likewise.

*Madeleine raised his head, met Javert's falcon eye still fixed upon him, looked at the motionless peasants, and smiled sadly. Then, without saying a word, he fell on his knees, and before the crowd had even had time to utter a cry, he was underneath the vehicle.*

# Week 2 – Day 7

Questions for personal reflection or group discussion

Keyword for the week: Responsibility

**Setting the scene**
Watch the DVD (8 minutes)
Start: Scene 3 Javert rides into Montreuil-Sur-Mer (13:45)
Finish: "Forgive me, Sir, I would not dare" (21:28)

**i 2 i**
*Issues to explore*
What stood out for you from this week's readings or movie clip?
Was there anything you didn't understand?
*Irritants*
Was there anything in the material with which you disagreed?

**The Day 6 Dilemma**
The struggle that comes from being a person created in the image
of God

What did Valjean possess that could help Fauchelevent?
What did he need to do in order to help Fauchelevent?
What was pulling him in the opposite direction?
How do you think you might have responded in this situation or
that of the parable of the Good Samaritan?

**Living it out**

*For by the grace given me I say to every one of you: Do not think of
yourself more highly than you ought, but rather think of yourself
with sober judgment, in accordance with the faith God has
distributed to each of you. For just as each of us has one body with*

*many members, and these members do not all have the same function, so in Christ we, though many, form one body, and each member belongs to all the others. We have different gifts, according to the grace given to each of us. If your gift is prophesying, then prophesy in accordance with your faith; if it is serving, then serve; if it is teaching, then teach; if it is to encourage, then give encouragement; if it is giving, then give generously; if it is to lead, do it diligently; if it is to show mercy, do it cheerfully. (Romans 12:3-8)*

How would you define the following phrases?

'Think of yourself with sober judgment';

'Each member belongs to all the others';

'We have different gifts, according to the grace given to each of us'.

How do we discover the gifts that God has given us?

What are the factors that can hold us back from using the gifts that God has given us to help others? What measures can we take to overcome them?

"How can you hold back when you have the chance to do good?" Do these words apply to you?

**i 2 i**

*Insights*

What insights have you gained from this week's material?

*Implementation*

Did you resolve to change anything in your life? What steps do you need to take to achieve this?

# 3

# Truth

*At each instant, gleams of the true came to complete his reason.*

# Week 3 – Day I

*Read Mark 7:14-23*

Fantine, as we have seen, has returned to Montreuil-Sur-Mer and found work in Valjean's factory. She is happy for the first time in a long while. She has a regular income, is able to rent a small room and furnish it, albeit on credit. She looks forward to being able to bring Cosette to be with her.

Then disaster strikes. Firstly, the Thenardiers, always looking to extract as much profit as possible, increase the monthly rate from seven francs to twelve and then to fifteen. The real danger, though, does not come from a rogue but from a Christian.

The gossips are always out in force when there is any hint of a mystery. It is noted that, at work, Fantine is occasionally tearful. It is also noted that she pays to have at least two letters written each month to the innkeeper at Montfermeil. The gossips line up alongside those who are just plain jealous of Fantine's blonde hair and shining teeth.

The letter writer is plied with alcohol and reveals Fantine's secret. Enter one Madame Victurnien, pillar of the church; owner of a small property which she had 'bequeathed with much osten-tation to a religious community'; friend of the Bishop of Arras; and inflexible guardian of public morals. Determined to get to the bottom of it she makes the trip to Montfermeil and proclaims, 'It cost me thirty-five francs but now I know everything. I've seen the child'.

Fantine had been at the factory for more than a year, when, one morning, the superintendent overseer handed her fifty francs from the mayor, told her that she was no longer employed in the factory, and requested her, in the mayor's name, to leave the neighborhood. This was the very month when the Thenardiers, after having demanded twelve francs instead of seven, had just exacted fifteen francs instead of twelve.

*Fantine was overwhelmed. She could not leave the neighborhood; she was in debt for her rent and furniture. Fifty francs was not sufficient to cancel this debt. She stammered a few supplicating words. The superintendent ordered her to leave the factory on the instant. Besides, Fantine was only a moderately good workwoman. Overcome with shame, even more than with despair, she quit the factory, and returned to her room. Her fault was now known to everyone.*

*She no longer felt strong enough to say a word. She was advised to see the mayor; she did not dare. The mayor had given her fifty francs because he was good, and had dismissed her because he was just. She bowed before the decision.*

In Valjean's defense he knows nothing of this. The overseer has exercised her authority in accordance with the principles that Valjean has laid down.

Madame Victurnien thought that she had established and confirmed the truth about Fantine but what is truth? To take a dictionary definition it is the state of being true, conforming to fact or reality. The problem is that even such solid things as fact and reality can depend on how we look at them. As an example, take the statement that 2 + 2 = 4 which is often used as an illustration of factual accuracy. In mathematical terms, that only holds because we are working in a decimal (base 10) system. If you are working in a base 3 system, 2 + 2 = 11! This immediately presents a challenge. We can talk about striving after absolute truth but each of us will have our own subjective perception of truth based upon our experience, value and belief systems.

Jesus certainly didn't try to win friends and influence people. On one occasion he was talking to some of the Jewish people who believed in him (John 8). They spoke of being children of Abraham but he lambasted them for being children of a rather different father. Their father, he said, was Satan, the father of lies. How could there be such a gulf between these devout Jews and

Jesus? Both believed in and claimed to follow the one true God. Both believed in the Law as God's guidance for humanity. The difference lay not in the raw data but in its interpretation.

Jesus takes this a stage further in discussing the Jewish food and cleanliness laws. The disciples had been criticized by the Pharisees for eating with 'unclean' hands because their hands had not been washed in the manner required by the Law. Jesus' teaching gets right to the heart of what really affects our relationship with God. He says that nothing that come from outside can make us unclean. The reason? Our relationship with God depends upon the state of our hearts. Any food we eat comes into the mouth, through the digestive system, into the stomach and then out. It doesn't touch the heart. What we should be worrying about instead, says Jesus, are those base emotions and motivations that are able to lodge in our hearts. These are the filter through which all of the everyday things in life are passed and by which we establish our perception of truth and act upon it. Their influence can result in all manner of evil actions. Jesus lists a few – evil thoughts, sexual immorality, theft, murder, adultery, greed, malice, deceit, lewdness, envy, slander, arrogance and folly.

Every day we have to deal with the raw material of life. What do we do with it? How we filter it and live our lives will depend upon what is in our hearts. How do we make sure that our perception of truth is as close to absolute truth as possible? Can we even say that there is such a thing as absolute truth?

Absolute truth does exist but in a person rather than anything that can be definitively written down. Jesus Christ is the way, the truth and the life. Our perception of truth will be closest to absolute truth the closer the contents of our hearts are to his. All Madame Victurnien had discovered was facts. Her heart was bigoted and twisted. As a result her actions had evil conse-quences. Had her heart been different she might have seen the truth.

# Week 3 – Day 2

*Read Mark 8:27-33*

Fantine begins a slow descent into utter misery. Through it all her only concern is Cosette and ensuring that her daughter is not thrown out on to the street. She is stuck between the proverbial rock and hard place. She is unable to find employment but cannot leave the town to look for work because the furniture dealer to whom she owes money threatens to have her arrested if she tries to leave the neighborhood. Despite returning all of the furniture except for a bed, she still owes one hundred francs.

The only work that she can find is piecework sewing which barely covers the exorbitant demands that the Thenardiers are now making. Nevertheless at least one person is happy:

> *Madame Victurnien sometimes saw her passing, from her window, noticed the distress of 'that creature' who, 'thanks to her,' had been 'put back in her proper place,' and congratulated herself. The happiness of the evil-minded is black.*

Fantine is becoming exhausted through a combination of long hours, eating very little and an already weakened chest. The bed goes to be replaced by a mattress and tattered blanket. All the while demands from her creditors and from the Thenardiers (who are now faking illnesses and sending her the medical bills) are growing. She sells her hair; she sells her teeth but all to no avail. Eventually she is forced into selling the only thing she has left to sell – her body. For her daughter's sake she becomes a prostitute.

Victor Hugo's comments at this point were written some 150 years ago but don't seem a moment out of place:

> *What is this history of Fantine? It is society purchasing a slave. From whom? From misery. From hunger, cold, isolation, destitution.*

*... A soul for a morsel of bread. Misery offers; society accepts.*

*The sacred law of Jesus Christ governs our civilization, but it does not, as yet, permeate it; it is said that slavery has disappeared from European civilization. This is a mistake. It still exists; but it weighs only upon the woman, and it is called prostitution. It weighs upon the woman, that is to say, upon grace, weakness, beauty, maternity. This is not one of the least of man's disgraces. At the point in this melancholy drama which we have now reached, nothing is left to Fantine of that which she had formerly been. She has become marble in becoming mire. Whoever touches her feels cold. She passes; she endures you; she ignores you; she is the severe and dishonored figure. Life and the social order have said their last word for her. All has happened to her that will happen to her. She has felt everything, borne everything, experienced everything, suffered everything, lost everything, mourned everything. She is resigned, with that resignation which resembles indifference, as death resembles sleep.*

One has to feel desperately sorry for Fantine. All she has ever wanted to do is to make a decent life for herself and her daughter but she is continually undermined. She was undermined by Tholomyes who abandoned her in Paris. She was undermined by the grasping Thenardiers. She was undermined by the bigoted busybody Madame Victurnien. She was undermined by the lack of communication at the factory. And, if we are honest, she was undermined by her own lousy decision-making.

Fantine's naivety keeps getting her into trouble. When she first met Tholomyes and linked up with the other three couples it seems very strange that she could not spot the 'business arrangement' to which everyone else was playing. Instead she gets herself pregnant at the outset. Then, on the road out of Paris, she gives away her daughter on a whim to a couple she has never met before and knows nothing about. When she gets to Montreuil-Sur-Mer, she makes what turns out to be the fatal mistake of over-extending herself on credit. And finally, when she is sacked from the factory and advised to appeal to Valjean, she decides to do nothing.

I think it is safe to say that Fantine is not the sharpest knife in the drawer but there are other factors at play. Remember Fantine's childhood, how she was found playing in the street as a young girl with no memory of father or mother. I can't help thinking that she had a strong desire to put that right and be part of a happy family. It blinds her to the real motives of Tholomyes. It persuades her to believe in the idyllic family scene at Montfermeil and want her daughter to be part of that. It leads her into imprudent choices as she feathers a nest for herself and Cosette in Montreuil-Sur-Mer. Our desires are powerful things and, if we're not careful, they can blind us to the proper course of action. In Mark's account of the parable of the sower (Mark 4), it is desires along with worry and the pursuit of wealth that can choke the growing word of God within us and Paul contrasts our human desires, those of the sinful nature, with those that are Spirit-inspired (Romans 8).

At Caesarea Philippi, Peter comes out with the cracking realization that Jesus really is the Messiah. His next statement, though, has Jesus rebuking him for being the mouthpiece of Satan. It is all because Peter's desires for Jesus are not tuned in to God's reality. His dreams are that Jesus will act in power to transform the nation. It is not surprising therefore that he rebels against talk of Jesus suffering and being rejected and killed.

Satan is never far away when our desires threaten to lead us awry and his fingerprints are also all over Fantine's failure to appeal. Satan the 'father of all lies' will do all that he can to destroy our lives with the wrong choices, whilst Satan the accuser will visit us in our distress to pile on the guilt and self-loathing. Why did Fantine not seek out Valjean? Because a little satanic voice whispered in her ear that she had brought it upon herself and deserved everything that was happening to her.

Don't listen to that voice when it speaks to you. The voice of

God by contrast is always gracious and restoring. I pray that the words of an old hymn may be always on our lips – Breathe through the heats of our desire, O still small voice of calm.

# Week 3 – Day 3

*Read Luke 11:14-22*

It is January 1823 and Fantine is soliciting for business in the snow. A young man, hanging around with nothing better to do, thinks it amusing to blow cigar smoke in her direction and, when this does not provoke a reaction, forces a handful of snow down her back between the bare shoulders.

This does provoke her and she launches herself at him, screaming and swearing and scratching at his face. A crowd forms to watch. At that moment, a tall man breaks through the crowd and seizes Fantine. Inspector Javert has made an arrest.

Justice in such a situation could be swiftly administered by the police. Javert is clear about what he has seen – a respectable member of society being attacked by somebody outside of society – and sentences Fantine to six months in jail. Fantine pleads with him to be merciful– she isn't that kind of a woman, she has a child, she owes money – but all to no avail.

Then Valjean enters the police post. Fantine spits in his face, believing him to be the cause of all her suffering. She rails against the injustice of it all but, this time, Valjean is there as her savior. He, like Javert, has only witnessed the end of the incident but has interviewed the bystanders and discovered the young man's fault. He commands Javert to set Fantine free. Javert refuses but Valjean reminds him that, although this is a police matter, the mayor may act as judge and is the higher authority.

Fantine is left in a state of utter confusion.

*She had just seen herself a subject of dispute between two opposing powers. She had seen two men who held in their hands her liberty, her life, her soul, her child, in combat before her very eyes; one of these men was drawing her towards darkness, the other was leading her back towards the light. In this conflict, viewed through* the exaggerations of terror, these two men had appeared to her like two giants; the one spoke like her demon, the other like her good angel.

The angel had conquered the demon, and, strange to say, that which made her shudder from head to foot was the fact that this angel, this liberator, was the very man whom she abhorred, that mayor whom she had so long regarded as the author of all her woes, that Madeleine! And at the very moment when she had insulted him in so hideous a fashion, he had saved her! Had she, then, been mistaken? Must she change her whole soul? She did not know; she trembled. She listened in bewilderment, she looked on in affright, and at every word uttered by M. Madeleine she felt the frightful shades of hatred crumble and melt within her, and something warm and ineffable, indescribable, which was both joy, confidence and love, dawn in her heart.

When Javert had taken his departure, M. Madeleine turned to her and said to her in a deliberate voice, like a serious man who does not wish to weep and who finds some difficulty in speaking: "I have heard you. I knew nothing about what you have mentioned. I believe that it is true, and I feel that it is true. I was even ignorant of the fact that you had left my shop. Why did you not apply to me? But here; I will pay your debts, I will send for your child, or you shall go to her. You shall live here, in Paris, or where you please. I undertake the care of your child and yourself. You shall not work any longer if you do not like. I will give all the money you require. You shall be honest and happy once more. And listen! I declare to you that if all is as you say, and I do not doubt it, you have never ceased to be virtuous and holy in the sight of God. Oh! Poor woman."

This was more than Fantine could bear. To have Cosette! To leave this life of infamy. To live free, rich, happy, respectable with Cosette; to see all these realities of paradise blossom of a sudden in the midst of her misery. She stared stupidly at this man who was talking to her, and could only give vent to two or three sobs, "Oh! Oh! Oh!" Her limbs gave way beneath her, she knelt in front of M.

*Madeleine, and before he could prevent her he felt her grasp his hand and press her lips to it.*
*Then she fainted.*

The picture that Victor Hugo paints, of an angel and a demon fighting over a soul, could have come from medieval art but it is not a New Testament picture. The authority of Jesus far exceeds anything else either now or forever (Ephesians 1:21).

How did people explain Jesus' great power to heal and perform miracles? For those whose starting point was a refusal to believe that Jesus was acting in God's name, there could be only one conclusion. It could only be that Jesus' power came from being in league with the Devil. Jesus met them head on. It was crazy, he said, to suggest that anyone using demonic powers would cast out demons. That would mean that Satan's kingdom was divided against itself and falling apart. Instead, Jesus points to a different reality. He is able to perform such miracles because the Devil is powerless to stand against him. The only person able to break through the armed defenses of a strong man is an even stronger one. Jesus is just such a person.

The Devil may try to convince you otherwise but if you are a Christian then he can have no hold over you. Just as Valjean had authority in the case of Fantine, so Jesus Christ has authority over your life. The Devil will still try to play with your mind but he cannot possess you. Like Fantine, you have been saved. You are a new creation. You are a saint.

## Week 3 — Day 4

*Read Luke 4:1-13*

Not long after the arrest and release of Fantine, Javert walks into Valjean's office. He announces that a serious offense has been committed. An 'inferior member of the public service has shown the utmost disrespect for a magistrate'. He is that person and furthermore it is too serious a matter for a mere resignation. He must be dismissed.

He goes on to explain the situation. He had suspected that the mayor was an escaped convict, Jean Valjean. Several things had given him this impression including the rescue of Fauchelevent. So certain had he been that he reported his suspicions to the police in Paris who laughed at him and said he was mad. Now he knows that he was wrong.

Then comes a bombshell, the reason why Javert had to be mistaken. The real Jean Valjean has been arrested stealing apples. He is in the prison at Arras having been living virtually destitute under the name of Champmathieu. Investigations have proved that thirty years previously he had been working as a tree pruner. Clearly he has put together his Christian name, Jean, with his mother's maiden name of Mathieu to form his new alias. Javert has been to see him and confirmed that he is indeed Jean Valjean, as have several of his former fellow prisoners. The trial is to take place the following day.

It is not difficult to imagine the mental torment that this news causes in Valjean's mind and we are presented with a very human picture:

*It would be beautiful, no doubt, after the bishop's holy words, after so many years of repentance and abnegation, in the midst of a penitence admirably begun, if this man had not flinched for an instant, even in the presence of so terrible a conjecture, but had continued to walk with the same step towards this yawning precipice, at the bottom of which lay heaven; that would have been beautiful; but it was not thus.*

As the hours pass, his mind goes over and over the dilemma. He arrives at different conclusions.

- This will, at last, bring security. I can escape the horror of a return to prison because there is a substitute to go in my place. Javert will probably clear off too. I don't have to lie. All I have to do is keep my mouth shut. Clearly God has caused this to happen. We must let God have his way.

- He asks himself 'What is my life's purpose?'

  *To conceal his name? To deceive the police? Was it for so petty a thing that he had done all that he had done? Had he not another and a grand object, which was the true one – to save, not his person, but his soul; to become honest and good once more; to be a just man? Was it not that above all, that alone, which he had always desired, which the bishop had enjoined upon him, to shut the door on his past? But he was not shutting it! great God! he was re-opening it by committing an infamous action! He was becoming a thief once more, and the most odious of thieves! He was robbing another of his existence, his life, his peace, his place in the sunshine. He was becoming an assassin. He was murdering, morally murdering, a wretched man.*

  Therefore, I must hand myself in.

- What about Fantine and Cosette and everyone who depends on me? If I go to prison all will be lost. In another ten years I could earn another ten million francs. Imagine the good that could do. After all, this Champmathieu's probably a rogue and may deserve to go to prison.

Finally, his conscience chips in again:

*That is good! Be an honest man yourself; remain Monsieur le Maire; remain honorable and honored; enrich the town; nourish the indigent; rear the orphan; live happy, virtuous, and admired; and, during this time, while you are here in the midst of joy and light, there will be a man who will wear your red blouse, who will bear your name in ignominy, and who will drag your chain in the galleys. Yes, it is well arranged thus. Ah, wretch!*

*Jean Valjean, there will be around you many voices, which will make a great noise, which will talk very loud, and which will bless you, and only one which no one will hear, and which will curse you in the dark. Well! listen, infamous man! All those benedictions will fall back before they reach heaven, and only the malediction will ascend to God.*

Sometimes the Devil's temptations can be very subtle as we struggle to work out the right thing to do. Jesus is pictured being led by the Holy Spirit into the desert for a time of reflection as his earthly ministry is beginning to unfold. Clearly, Satan is not going to waste an opportunity to play with Jesus' mind.

Jesus is hungry and so the Devil tempts him to turn stones into bread. Our physical well-being and security will always be important to us. This was the first thing that Valjean thought about as the name 'Jean Valjean' brought back terrible memories. Jesus' response? It may be important but more important is listening to what God wants us to do.

Jesus is offered all power and authority in the world. It is not hard to imagine, as Valjean does, all the good that could flow from so much influence. Surely this must count for something. Jesus' response? Don't be misled. Worship God and serve him alone.

Finally, Jesus is taken to the highest point of the temple. Throw yourself off, says the Devil, and no harm will come to you. God will protect you – You're his son.

Valjean too is tempted with the thought that he has changed. He is virtuous. He is God's child. God is looking after him. Therefore, this must be God's protection upon him which can be proved by his doing nothing and surviving. Jesus' response? It is never right to put God to the test.

As Valjean's conscience reminds him, what good is it for someone to gain a life but lose a soul.

## Week 3 – Day 5

*Read Mark 14:32-42*

Valjean's torment continues. He rises early on the day of the trial resolved to go to Arras even though it's not what his heart wants him to do. On the way out of Montreuil-Sur-Mer, however, he bangs against the post-cart and, when he stops to rest, discovers that one of the wheels is too badly damaged to continue. There is no prospect of its being repaired that day and there is seemingly no chance of obtaining another vehicle.

> *It was evident that Providence was intervening. That it was it who had broken the wheel of the Tilbury and who was stopping him on the road. He had not seen this at first. He had just made every possible effort to continue the journey; he had loyally and scrupu-lously exhausted all means; he had been deterred neither by the season, nor fatigue, nor by the expense; he had nothing with which to reproach himself. If he went no further, that was no fault of his. It did not concern him further. It was no longer his fault. It was not the act of his own conscience, but the act of Providence. He breathed again. He breathed freely and to the full extent of his lungs for the first time since Javert's visit. It seemed to him that the hand of iron which had held his heart in its grasp for the last twenty hours had just released him. It seemed to him that God was for him now, and was manifesting Himself. He said himself that he had done all he could, and that now he had nothing to do but retrace his steps quietly.*

At that point he discovers that there is, after all, a small carriage available. He restarts his journey but again disaster strikes. The crosspiece breaks but Valjean is able to improvise, using the branch of a tree. When he finally arrives in Arras it is eight o'clock, two hours after the Court usually finishes for the day.

72

Nevertheless there are still shining lights and people inside. He is informed that the case is over. Asking about the verdict he is told that there has been a conviction and a sentence of hard labor for life. Only then does he discover that it is not his trial. Champmathieu's trial is still in progress.

He tries to enter the courtroom but is refused entry as the court is full. By revealing his identity as Mayor of Montreuil-Sur-Mer he is given special permission by the judge to attend the case. An usher shows him into the judges' room. All he has to do, he is told, is to go to the door on the other side of the room, open it and he will be in the courtroom. He paces. He frets. He attempts to flee. He spends fifteen minutes in intense deliberation. Then he opens the door and walks through it.

It is not difficult to pick out the accused:

*He thought he was looking at himself, grown old; not absolutely the same in face, of course, but exactly similar in attitude and aspect, with his bristling hair, with that wild and uneasy eye, with that blouse, just as it was on the day when he entered Digne, full of hatred, concealing his soul in that hideous mass of frightful thoughts which he had spent nineteen years in collecting on the floor of the prison. He said to himself with a shudder, "Good God! Shall I become like that again?"*

There may still be hope of a reprieve if Champmathieu is found not guilty but very soon even this hope is dashed. It is clear that Champmathieu is a simple peasant of limited intelligence who really does not understand what is going on. His defense team are not much better, choosing to fight the charge of stealing apples whilst accepting the identification as Jean Valjean as a fait accompli. There is only going to be one possible outcome. Instead Valjean stands up and proclaims, *"I am the man you are looking for. I am Jean Valjean."*

We can only begin to imagine the torment that was going

through Jesus' mind in the Garden of Gethsemane. He knew that potentially painful and life-threatening events were awaiting him. All he wanted to do was remain faithful to God but, like Valjean, he must have been desperately hoping that there would be a last minute reprieve to save him. Hence his words, "Abba, Father, everything is possible for you. Take this cup from me. Yet not what I will, but what you will." This was no robot, programmed to go to the cross and bring us salvation. This was a human being just like us, suffering such torture that Luke describes his sweat falling as drops of blood to the ground.

On October 31 1517, Martin Luther famously nailed his 95 Theses to the university door in Wittenberg in an act that would lead to the Protestant Reformation. Four years later, on April 17 1521, he appeared before the Diet of Worms. He was presented with a list of his writings and asked (a) whether he was the author and (b) whether he still stood by the contents. His answer to the former was immediate but he requested a day to consider his answer to the second question. He knew the enormity of what he was being asked to do both for his own safety and for the likely impact on the church. History has usually painted him determined and steadfast but this too was a man who whiled away the night hours in mental agonies. He prayed and consulted with others. He knew the path along which God was leading him but really did not want to take it if there was a God-given alternative available.

There are times in our Christian lives when we follow in the footsteps of Jesus, Martin Luther and Jean Valjean. God leads us down a painful path we would rather not tread. If you are in that place today, may God grant you strength and courage and may your response be that of Jesus – not my will but yours.

# Week 3 – Day 6

*Read John 18:28-40*

What has happened to Fantine in the period since her arrest and release? She has been taken to the factory infirmary where two nuns, Sister Perpetua and Sister Simplice, are caring for her. Fantine's illness is never named but Hugo appears to be describing the effects of tuberculosis, the scourge of the urban poor. Her condition is deteriorating and the doctor advises that Cosette should be brought to her sooner rather than later. The Thenardiers, though, are not playing ball. Fantine owes them two hundred and twenty francs so Valjean sends three hundred, asking them to take Cosette's traveling expenses to Montreuil-Sur-Mer from the balance.

Thenardier realizes that Cosette has become a goldmine and sends a bill for fake medical expenses amounting to another three hundred francs. This is paid but still the Thenardiers hold on to Cosette, giving numerous reasons why she cannot be sent. Finally, Valjean decides that he or somebody else must go in person. That is the point at which Javert tells him about Champmathieu's trial in Arras.

Who is Sister Simplice? She is a woman given to total honesty:

*However pure and sincere we may be, we all bear upon our candor the crack of the little, innocent lie. She did not. Little lie, innocent lie – does such a thing exist? To lie is the absolute form of evil. To lie a little is not possible: he who lies, lies the whole lie. To lie is the very face of the demon. Satan has two names; he is called Satan and Lying. That is what she thought; and as she thought, so she did. The result was the whiteness which we have mentioned – a whiteness which covered even her lips and her eyes with radiance.*

When Valjean reveals his true identity there is confusion in the Arras courtroom and he takes the opportunity to slip away unnoticed and return home on the night post-coach. When Javert catches up with him he is at Fantine's bedside. Valjean begs for three days to go and fetch Cosette but, unsurprisingly, Javert refuses. It causes Fantine to realize that there is no hope of Cosette's imminent arrival and that, with Valjean arrested, her savior is gone. In her weakened state the shock is sufficient to kill her. She is twenty-seven years old.

Valjean is put into the town's prison from which he escapes and returns to his room in the factory. He leaves some money and writes a note for the priest, asking him to pay for Fantine's funeral and the expenses of the trial with the remainder to go to the poor. Only Sister Simplice knows that he is there.

When Javert arrives he finds the nun kneeling in prayer. Unbeknown to him, Valjean is hiding behind the door.

*This was Sister Simplice, who had never told a lie in her life. Javert knew it, and held her in special veneration in consequence. "Sister," said he, "are you alone in this room?" A terrible moment ensued, during which the poor servant felt as though she should faint.*

*The sister raised her eyes and answered: "Yes."*

*"Then," resumed Javert, "you will excuse me if I persist; it is my duty; you have not seen a certain person – a man – this evening? He has escaped; we are in search of him – that Jean Valjean; you have not seen him?"*

*The sister replied: "No." She lied. She had lied twice in succession, one after the other, without hesitation, promptly, as a person does when sacrificing herself.*

*"Pardon me," said Javert, and he retired with a deep bow.*

As Pontius Pilate interviews Jesus, he is face to face with absolute truth in human form yet he reveals a different take on truth. It is revealed in the cynical question "What is truth?" and in the decision to leave Jesus' fate to the mob despite having found him innocent. For Pilate, truth has more to do with pragmatism than morality. The end justifies the means. What about Sister Simplice? Is she a Pilate placing practical considerations ahead of moral ones or are there situations in which we can justify lying in the name of a higher truth?

In the book *From the Prophet's Pen*, Arthur Wallis recounts the story of a Dutch lady whose experience during the Second World War mirrors that of Sister Simplice. Her family provided sanctuary for Jews and other wanted people. One day she was stopped by some German soldiers and asked at gunpoint whether anyone was being hidden in her house. Like Sister Simplice, she lied and said no with the result that several lives were saved. Was she right to do so?

Wallis' analysis of this situation has pricked me over the years. He argues that God commands us not to lie and that this is an absolute. We have the right to remain silent but we should not lie. To do otherwise is to seize control from God.

*"God alone is the source of all good. Man cannot be righteous or act righteously except in relationship with God. On this basis what may appear to human judgment a fine and noble act may be either worthless or positively evil in the estimate of God. ... We should view that young Dutch girl's agonizing dilemma with the utmost compassion. In her position we might well have done the same. But this should not cloud the issue. 'To God, the Lord, belongs escape from death' (Psalm 68:20 RSV). We are not required to try to effect by unrighteous means what we fear he may be unwilling to do."*

The whole of my being wants to disagree with him. I want to argue that there is a greater truth than the 'correctness' of mere words. But, if I'm honest, I haven't yet found peace one way or the other. I'll leave the dilemma with you.

There is one sad postscript to report. Fantine was treated in death as in life:

*The priest thought that he was doing right, and perhaps he really was, in reserving as much money as possible from what Jean Valjean had left for the poor. Who was concerned, after all? A convict and a woman of the town. That is why he had a very simple funeral for Fantine, and reduced it to that strictly necessary form known as the pauper's grave. So Fantine was buried in the free corner of the cemetery which belongs to anybody and everybody, and where the poor are lost. Fortunately, God knows where to find the soul again.*

# Week 3 – Day 7

Questions for personal reflection or group discussion

Keyword for the week: Truth

## Setting the scene
Watch the DVD (17 minutes)
Start: Scene 4 Fantine walking in the dark (21:28)
Finish: "You will find me at the hospital" (38:34)

## i 2 i
*Issues to explore*
What stood out for you from this week's readings or movie clip?
Was there anything you didn't understand?
*Irritants*
Was there anything in the material with which you disagreed?

## The Day 6 Dilemma
The struggle that comes from being a person created in the image of God

Why do you think Sister Simplice lied?
Would you have lied in her situation or that of the Dutch girl?
Do you believe that she was right to lie?

## Living it out

*Therefore, I urge you, brothers and sisters, in view of God's mercy, to offer your bodies as a living sacrifice, holy and pleasing to God – this is your true and proper worship. Do not conform to the pattern of this world, but be transformed by the renewing of your mind. Then you will be able to test and approve what God's will is – his good, pleasing and perfect will. ... Love must be sincere. Hate what is evil; cling to what is good. (Romans 12:1-2 and 9)*

In different ways, Madame Victurnien, Fantine and Javert all failed to see the truth of the situations in which they found themselves. Why do you think this was?

What was it that enabled Valjean to see the truth of what he had to do?

Paul asks us to be transformed by the renewing of our minds and to love with a sincere love that hates all things evil. How will this advice help us to stay in tune with truth?

**i 2 i**

*Insights*

What insights have you gained from this week's material?

*Implementation*

Did you resolve to change anything in your life? What steps do you need to take to achieve this?

# 4

# Compassion

*Forests are apocalypses; and the beating of the wings of a little soul makes an agonizing sound under their monstrous vault.*

# Week 4 – Day 1

*Read Matthew 18:1-14*

After leaving Sister Simplice and the factory, Valjean withdraws his savings and goes to Paris. Three days later he is arrested boarding the coach to Montfermeil. His money is never found, although the road mender of Montfermeil had caught sight of a mysterious person digging in the woods near the village. Valjean is returned to Toulon prison to continue his sentence. Four months later, he is involved in an 'accident' when he falls from the top of a tall mast having rescued a sailor. He is presumed drowned but his body, like his money, is never found.

Cosette is now eight years old. Her life with the Thenardiers has been one of complete misery. The first thing that the Thenardiers did, upon Fantine's departure, was to pawn Cosette's fine wardrobe. From that day on she has been dressed in rags. Any clothes that Fantine sends are given to their own children. Cosette is fed on leftovers which she has to eat with the cat and the dog from a wooden bowl under the table.

By the age of three, Cosette is enduring physical violence and abuse:

*Cosette could not make a motion which did not draw down upon her head a heavy shower of violent blows and unmerited chastisement. The sweet, feeble being, who should not have understood anything of this world or of God, incessantly punished, scolded, ill-used, beaten, and seeing beside her two little creatures like herself, who lived in a ray of dawn!*

By the age of five she has become the family's slave. She rises early and spends the day on household chores. Local people, knowing nothing of Fantine's payments, assume from her rags that she is a charity case taken in out of kindness. They nickname her 'The Lark' because she is always up before dawn but this is 'a lark that never sings'.

*Like all children, who resemble young shoots of the vine, which cling to everything, she had tried to love; she had not succeeded. All had repulsed her, the Thenardiers, their children, other children. She had loved the dog, and he had died, after which nothing and nobody would have anything to do with her. It is a sad thing to say, and we have already intimated it, that, at eight years of age, her heart was cold. It was not her fault; it was not the faculty of loving that she lacked; alas! it was the possibility.*

At the age of eight:

*Her entire clothing was but a rag which would have inspired pity in summer, and which inspired horror in winter. All she had on was hole-ridden linen, not a scrap of woolen. Her skin was visible here and there and everywhere black and blue spots could be descried, which marked the places where the Thenardier woman had touched her. Her naked legs were thin and red. The hollows in her neck were enough to make one weep. This child's whole person, her mien, her attitude, the sound of her voice, the intervals which she allowed to elapse between one word and the next, her glance, her silence, her slightest gesture, expressed and betrayed one sole idea – fear.*

It all began with a question about status. The disciples asked the question, "Who is the greatest in the Kingdom of Heaven?" They must have been surprised at Jesus' response. He took a child and held him up as a role model. His point? Well, have you ever watched a young child at Christmas? It's a chastening experience. They're not interested in the size of the presents or how much each one cost. Give them the empty boxes and the discarded wrapping paper and they'll play all day. That trait continues in various ways throughout childhood. They simply aren't interested in the adult concept of status. Jesus says that we will never amount to much in the Kingdom unless we learn to look at the world in the same way.

And then he goes on to say some remarkable things.

- Whoever welcomes a little child welcomes me.

- Anyone who causes one of these little ones to sin can expect the worst (I paraphrase).

- Their angels see the face of my Father in Heaven.

- My Father in Heaven does not want any of these little ones to be lost.

The third of these statements is the most remarkable. Whenever Jesus mentions angels elsewhere it is in the context of Heaven or the End Times. This is the only time that he links angels to specific people.

When my son was three we took him to an evening service at a church we had never been to before. We were made to feel very welcome and given special seats at the back of the large hall in which the church was meeting, so that our son could move around if necessary. These were several yards away from the official back row of seats. Our son busied himself on his mother's lap, reading books, talking to himself and asking the occasional question. His behavior, for a three year old, was very good. One or two people looked round occasionally but out of what looked like curiosity rather than disdain. Imagine our surprise therefore when, thirty minutes into the sermon (and with the preacher exhorting his congregation to show mercy!), we were accosted by a gentleman we presume was the sound technician as he was wearing a black tee shirt and headphones. His words to us were these. "Get him out of here. He's disturbing everyone in the place."

Those words have left a far deeper impact on me than I might have expected. I have reflected upon my reaction. In part it is the response of a loving father to an attack upon his child. In part it is the thought of what effect those words of rejection have upon a three-year-old child. But, as I read these verses, I wonder too whether what I was tuning into was the outrage of the angels.

Cosette did not have a loving father to watch over her but she did have her supporters in Heaven. They knew that her savior was on his way.

# Week 4 – Day 2

*Read John 1:1-14*

It is Christmas Eve 1823. On the streets of Montfermeil is a collection of brightly lit stalls and sideshows, ready to catch people on their way to midnight mass. On one stall is a magnificent doll, nearly two-feet tall, at which Eponine and Azelma have spent hours gazing.

Inside the inn there is the usual mix of political debate and local gossip. Madame Thenardier is busy roasting a joint over the fire. Cosette is sitting in her usual place under the table knitting stockings for the Thenardier children. She is dressed in rags and her own feet are bare in their wooden clogs.

Madame Thenardier realizes they are out of water and Cosette prays for it to be morning. Fetching water will mean a walk to the spring in the woods. Her prayer goes unanswered. A guest's horse needs watering and Cosette is ordered out into the dark and cold. The bucket is bigger than she is.

Cosette crosses the road and is distracted by the doll:

*The whole shop seemed a palace to her: the doll was not a doll; it was a vision. It was joy, splendor, riches, happiness, which appeared in a sort of chimerical halo to that unhappy little being so profoundly engulfed in gloomy and chilly misery. With the sad and innocent sagacity of childhood, Cosette measured the abyss which separated her from that doll. She said to herself that one must be a queen, or at least a princess, to have a 'thing' like that.*

Her dreaming is interrupted by the yells of Madame Thenardier who has seen her. Cosette leaves the bright lights behind and trudges fearfully into the darkness of the wood. She is terrified by the thought of the wild animals and evil spirits that might be surrounding her. She starts to return home but her greater fear is of the wild and evil beast waiting there. She is on the brink of tears as she feels the immensity of the physical and spiritual darkness bearing down on her.

At last she comes to the spring and fills the bucket. It is now almost too heavy to lift.

*She panted with a sort of painful rattle; sobs contracted her throat, but she dared not weep, so afraid was she of the Thenardier, even at a distance: it was her custom to imagine the Thenardier always present. However, she could not make much headway in that manner, and she went on very slowly. In spite of diminishing the length of her stops, and of walking as long as possible between them, she reflected with anguish that it would take her more than an hour to return to Montfermeil in this manner, and that the Thenardier would beat her. This anguish was mingled with her terror at being alone in the woods at night; she was worn out with fatigue, and had not yet emerged from the forest. On arriving near an old chestnut tree with which she was acquainted, made a last halt, longer than the rest, in order that she might get well rested; then she summoned up all her strength, picked up her bucket again, and courageously resumed her march, but the poor little desperate creature could not refrain from crying, "O my God! My God!"*

*At that moment she suddenly became conscious that her bucket no longer weighed anything at all: a hand, which seemed to her enormous, had just seized the handle, and lifted it vigorously. She raised her head. A large black form, straight and erect, was walking beside her through the darkness; it was a man who had come up behind her and whose approach she had not heard. This man, without uttering a word, had seized the handle of the bucket which she was carrying. There are instincts for all the encounters of life. The child was not afraid.*

The hand belongs to Jean Valjean who accompanies her back to the inn.

*She no longer felt any fatigue. From time to time she raised her eyes towards the man, with a sort of tranquility and an indescribable confidence. She had never been taught to turn to Providence and to pray; nevertheless, she felt within her something which resembled hope and joy, and which mounted towards heaven.*

Valjean carries the bucket for Cosette but she insists on taking it the last few steps for fear of being beaten. She is soaked but too afraid to dry herself in front of the fire and goes straight back to her place under the table. Valjean arranges a night's lodging with the Thenardiers. They are struggling to work him out. He is dressed shabbily yet seems to have plenty of money. He pays for Cosette to stop knitting and, unnoticed, she begins to play with a doll abandoned by Eponine and Azelma. She has no doll of her own. She is discovered and rebuked at which point Valjean leaves the inn. He returns a few minutes later with the doll that all three of the girls have admired.

*Cosette raised her eyes; she gazed at the man approaching her with that doll as she might have gazed at the sun; she heard the unprecedented words, "It is for you"; she stared at him; she stared at the doll; then she slowly retreated, and hid herself at the extreme end, under the table in a corner of the wall.*

*"The gentleman has given you a doll, my little Cosette," said Thenardier, with a caressing air. "Take it; it is yours."*

*Cosette gazed at the marvelous doll in a sort of terror. Her face was still flooded with tears, but her eyes began to fill, like the sky at daybreak, with strange beams of joy. What she felt at that moment was a little like what she would have felt if she had been abruptly told, "Little one, you are the Queen of France."*

*"Truly, sir?" said Cosette. "Is it true? Is the 'lady' mine?"*

*The stranger's eyes seemed to be full of tears. He appeared to have reached that point of emotion where a man does not speak for fear lest he should weep. He nodded to Cosette, and placed the "lady's" hand in her tiny hand.*

It is Christmas and salvation has come into the darkness of Cosette's world.

# Week 4 – Day 3

*Read Matthew 13:31-33*

*Valjean*
Valjean, after dramatically finding Cosette in the woods at Montfermeil, pays off the Thenardiers and takes Cosette to Paris where they rent a small room as anonymously as possible. Unfortunately it is not anonymous enough. His charity is his undoing. An 'old' man dressed shabbily but giving generously to beggars is bound to have people talking.

*Valjean and Javert*
After Valjean's escape from prison, the police post Javert to Paris on the basis that it is a magnet for anyone on the run. Javert stays on after Valjean's recapture. He has proved himself so useful that the transfer is made permanent. He reads the account of Valjean's 'death' in the newspaper and presumes the matter closed. His eyes and ears though are always open. He sees reports of a little girl (Name: Cosette; Mother's name: Fantine) 'snatched' from Montfermeil. He makes the link to Montreuil-Sur-Mer and investigates but, by now, the Thenardiers have become more tight-lipped. Then he hears about the old man and a little girl who knows nothing except that she has come from Montfermeil. He dresses as a beggar and recognizes Valjean's face when he gives him money.

Ever wary, Valjean also recognizes Javert's face and that night a police patrol led by Javert chases Valjean and Cosette through the streets of Paris.

*Jean Valjean knew no more where he was going than did Cosette. He trusted in God, as she trusted in him. It seemed as though he also were clinging to the hand of someone greater than himself; he thought he felt a being leading him, though invisible.*

Eventually, Javert has his prey surrounded in a warren of back streets. Slowly, the net tightens as the patrol moves in. The trapped Valjean calls once again upon his prodigious strength. With Cosette on his back he scales a tall wall and finds himself in … a convent. That is not the only surprise. The convent's gardener turns out to be Fauchelevent, the man Valjean rescued from underneath his cart and in the employment that Valjean had arranged for him.

The police are thwarted in their hunt. Valjean and Cosette spend the next five years in the convent. Valjean, posing as Fauchelevent's brother and now going under the name of Ultime Fauchelevent, is taken on to the gardening staff. Cosette is installed in the convent school and educated with the other girls.

Valjean and Cosette finally emerge from the convent in 1829 upon Fauchelevent's death. They continue to live in Paris, keeping as low a profile as possible and maintaining three houses in case the police ever catch up with them again.

*The Thenardiers*
The Thenardiers' business in Montfermeil fails not long after Cosette's departure and they too come to Paris. They spend at least one winter sleeping rough and the next time we shall meet them they will be living in a hovel. Thenardier gets involved with the Parisian criminal underworld.

It could be tempting to see these first years in Paris as inactive years. There is the odd escapade but one gets the sense that the main action is on hold. Nevertheless this is a crucial period in Valjean's journey.

In his relationship with Cosette he discovers, for the first time, a love that is more than just Christian duty.

*Jean Valjean had never loved anything; for twenty-five years he had been alone in the world. He had never been father, lover, husband, friend. In the prison he had been vicious, gloomy, chaste, ignorant, and shy. ... When he saw Cosette, when he had taken possession of her, carried her off, and delivered her, he felt his heart moved within him. All the passion and affection within him awoke, and rushed towards that child. He approached the bed, where she lay sleeping, and trembled with joy. He suffered all the pangs of a mother, and he knew not what it meant; for that great and singular movement of a heart which begins to love is a very obscure and a very sweet thing. Poor old man, with a perfectly new heart!*

*Only, as he was five and fifty, and Cosette eight years of age, all that might have been love in the whole course of his life flowed together into a sort of ineffable light.*

*It was the second white apparition which he had encountered. The bishop had caused the dawn of virtue to rise on his horizon; Cosette caused the dawn of love to rise.*

The convent too played its part.

*God has his own ways, moreover; the convent contributed, like Cosette, to uphold and complete the bishop's work in Jean Valjean. It is certain that virtue adjoins pride on one side. A bridge built by the devil exists there. Jean Valjean had been, unconsciously, perhaps, tolerably near that side and that bridge, when Providence cast his lot in the convent of the Petit-Picpus; so long as he had compared himself only to the bishop, he had regarded himself as unworthy and had remained humble; but for some time past he had been comparing himself to men in general, and pride was beginning to spring up. Who knows? He might have ended by returning very gradually to hatred. The convent stopped him on that downward path.*

Jesus used two everyday illustrations to illustrate the principles of spiritual growth in God's Kingdom. The first was of a tiny mustard seed that grows until it becomes the largest of plants able to provide shade and cover for the birds. The second is of a woman mixing yeast into dough so that it will rise. Both stories have a second factor in common beyond that of phenomenal growth. In each case there is a waiting time where growth is happening but unseen. A seed left in the ground takes time to push shoots above the surface of the soil. A batch of dough has to be left on one side until ready.

So it is with our Christian lives. Sometimes we have to go through periods of waiting where nothing much seems to be happening. Be patient if that is your experience right now. Remember that, as it was for Valjean, these may turn out to be some of the most valuable years of all.

# Week 4 – Day 4

*Read Luke 8:1-15*

We shall spend the next three days in the company of the Thenardier children. We have already met the two older children, Eponine and Azelma, at their parents' inn.

Azelma remains an undeveloped character whose greatest achievement is to survive to the end of the book. Eponine has a much larger role.

If Cosette was the Cinderella of Christmas 1823 then Eponine and Azelma are two beautiful sisters.

> *They were two really pretty little girls, more bourgeois than peasant in looks, and very charming; the one with shining chestnut tresses, the other with long black braids hanging down her back, both vivacious, neat, plump, rosy, and healthy, and a delight to the eye.*

By 1832, when Cosette has blossomed into her prime, all that has changed.

Victor Hugo uses the analogy of mining to describe the different strata that underlie the social order. Right at the bottom is 'the grave of shadows'. This is the domain of *les misérables*, most of whom, it is envisaged, will be led to some form of crime by absolute necessity.

> *The wild specters who roam in this grave, almost beasts, almost phantoms, are not occupied with universal progress; they are ignorant both of the idea and of the word; they take no thought for anything but the satisfaction of their individual desires. They are almost unconscious, and there exists within them a sort of terrible obliteration. They have two mothers, both step-mothers, ignorance and misery.*

Eponine is on the cusp between childhood and adulthood but she already has one foot in the grave of shadows. When we first meet her in Paris, she is pictured running through the mist like a ghoul. She has bloodshot specter-like eyes and when she performs an act of kindness for an old man, she is described as appearing so mysteriously that he mistakes her for a spirit or goblin.

> *"God will bless you," said he, "you are an angel since you take care of the flowers." "No," she replied. "I am the devil, but that's all the same to me."*

Eponine is now the one dressed in rags; the one going barefoot; the one whose hand 'is small, bony, and feeble as that of a skeleton'. She is still a child, not yet a woman, yet the circles in which her father mixes have stolen any innocence from her. She is her father's messenger, well used to running from the police. She is sexually active and her father does not appear averse to offering out her sexual favors to his own advantage. She sleeps under bridges, in haylofts as well as in the hovel that is home. Her chest rattles with a dry cough and she speaks with 'a dull, broken, hoarse, strangled voice, the voice of an old man, roughened with brandy and liquor'.

> *She was a frail, emaciated, slender creature; there was nothing but a chemise and a petticoat upon that chilled and shivering nakedness. Her girdle was a string, her head ribbon a string, her pointed shoulders emerged from her chemise, a blond and lymphatic pallor, earth-colored collar-bones, red hands, a half-open and degraded mouth, missing teeth, dull, bold, base eyes; she had the form of a young girl who has missed her youth, and the look of a corrupt old woman; fifty years mingled with fifteen; one of those beings which are both feeble and horrible, and which cause those to shudder whom they do not cause to weep.*

Among the Greek myths is the story of Pandora's Box. Pandora (whose name means 'all gifts') is the first created woman. She is given a container by the god Zeus which she is told she mustn't open. Curiosity gets the better of her and she releases the contents, all forms of evil and depravity, into the world. The only thing to remain in the box is hope.

Eponine is at the point where there is still hope. Debauchery has made its mark but there is enough of her underlying nature that is kind and warm. Even within her grotesque appearance, there remains some beauty trying to break out.

As the Gospel writers describe the crucifixion and resurrection they mention various women being present. The names change in each account with only one name appearing in all four gospels, that of Mary Magdalene. It is clear that Mary was part of Jesus' inner circle. It was not always that way. Luke reveals that there had been a time when Mary had been very different. She had been possessed by seven demons which should probably not be taken as a strict numerical tally but as an expression of the severity of her problem!

What would it have meant to be affected by seven demons? Luke does not provide any clues although elsewhere demon possession is characterized by violence of behavior. Clearly sevenfold possession implies some pretty serious stuff. I imagine that most people would have written her off but, even when you are afflicted by all the evils of the world, there can still be hope. Along came Jesus and with him came healing and restoration.

Luke follows up with Jesus' parable of the sower. It is a sobering thought that, if it can be sown, the seed of the gospel is more likely to flourish in the Marys and Eponines of this world than in far more respectable people. That's because the negative pulls of the parable have significantly less power. Once they've recognized it for what it is, it's much harder to prize the pearl of great price from a beggar who has nothing to lose.

Remember that the name Pandora means 'all gifts'. It's a

reminder that all of us enter life with so many of God's gifts inside us. We have so much potential. The circumstances of life and the actions of others can degrade us as they did Eponine but can never remove our God-given potential. There is always hope. Our job as Christians is to bring Jesus into the equation so that hope may be transformed into life in all its fullness.

How do you view the Eponines of this world when you meet them in the street? Do you see the debauchery or do you see the hope?

# Week 4 – Day 5

*Read Luke 18:15-25*

The Thenardiers have five children. We have already met Eponine and Azelma. The third child, and oldest boy, is called Gavroche whilst his two younger brothers are both unnamed. Madame Thenardier, as we have seen, is a fearsome character whose single redeeming feature (if it can be called that) is the love that she has for her girls. This love does not extend to her boys as can be seen from our first introduction to Gavroche at Montfermeil:

> At intervals the cry of a very young child, which was somewhere in the house, rang through the noise of the inn. It was a little boy who had been born to the Thenardiers during one of the preceding winters, "she did not know why," she said, "the result of the cold," and who was a little more than three years old. The mother had nursed him, but she did not love him. When the persistent clamor of the brat became too annoying, "Your son is squalling," Thenardier would say; "do go and see what he wants." "Bah!" the mother would reply, "he bothers me." And the neglected child continued to shriek in the dark.

By the time of Gavroche's next appearance he is eleven and in Paris. Like Eponine, his fortunes have changed:

> This child was well muffled up in a pair of man's trousers, but he did not get them from his father, and a woman's chemise, but he did not get it from his mother. Some people or other had clothed him in rags out of charity. Still, he had a father and a mother. But his father did not think of him, and his mother did not love him. He was one of those children most deserving of pity, among all, one of those who have father and mother, and who are orphans nevertheless. This

*child never felt so well as when he was in the street. The pavements were less hard to him than his mother's heart. His parents had dispatched him into life with a kick. He simply took flight. He was a boisterous, pallid, nimble, wide-awake, jeering, lad, with a vivacious but sickly air. He went and came, sang, played at hopscotch, scraped the gutters, stole a little, but, like cats and sparrows, gaily laughed when he was called a rogue, and got angry when called a thief. He had no shelter, no bread, no fire, no love; but he was merry because he was free.*

The origins of Mothering Sunday lie in one of the lectionary passages traditionally read on the middle Sunday of Lent. Paul, in Galatians 4, uses the Genesis story of the two sons born to Abraham, by his slave-girl Hagar and his wife Sarah. One, he says, was born ordinarily (to Hagar) whilst the other was born as a result of God's promise. Paul uses the two women as symbols of the old and new covenants.

*"Now Hagar stands for Mount Sinai in Arabia and corresponds to the present city of Jerusalem, because she is in slavery with her children. But the Jerusalem that is above is free, and she is our mother." (Galatians 4:25-26)*

First, the tradition grew up that on this Sunday one attended the local 'mother' church, i.e. the cathedral. By Victorian times the tradition had changed to require servant boys and girls to return to their families and attend their mother church i.e. the church their family attended. It was a day for catching up with loved ones; a day without work and a day for feasting as the usual restrictions of Lent were relaxed.

Gavroche knew no such luxuries. He very occasionally returned home but was not welcomed when he did. There was no family relationship to be enjoyed. He preferred to live on the streets where he could at least be free.

If Gavroche were alive today he would no doubt be viewed by society as an anti-social nuisance, yet he is also the proverbial street urchin with a heart of gold. It's as if, in his freedom and innocence, he instinctively knows the demands of the new covenant. He does not need to have them explained or demonstrated. Gavroche has a strong sense of justice. He helps out an old man with no money. He gives the cloak off his back – a woolen shawl actually – to a shivering beggar-girl. He even helps his enemies when help is needed.

People were bringing babies and children to Jesus to be blessed. We do not know specifically why they were doing this – although the high infant mortality rate may have had a lot to do with it – nor why the disciples were trying to turn them away. We do know Jesus' response: "Let the little children come to me, and do not hinder them, for the kingdom of God belongs to such as these." Children, like Gavroche, are nowhere near perfect but it is their intuitive qualities to which Jesus is alluding. These can disappear with the clutter of adulthood. It is no coincidence that the story is followed by the contrast of the wealthy ruler's question about what he needs to do to gain eternal life and Jesus' verdict that he needs to declutter himself of the material riches that surround him.

But Gavroche's most touching qualities are displayed when he takes under his wing two small boys that he finds lost on the streets. He buys them bread even though he himself hasn't eaten for three days. He provides them with shelter. He begins to tutor them in the ways of the street. He even tucks them into what passes for a bed and soothes their night-time fears with the assurances of a mother close at hand.

Gavroche may be a boy but he's more of a mother than his mother will ever be.

# Week 4 – Day 6

*Read Luke 16:19-31*

We turn now to the final two Thenardier children, the two unnamed boys, who we have met already without realizing it. There are many tragic stories in the book but theirs is perhaps the most tragic. These are the two small boys that Gavroche took under his wing. He had no idea that they were family although to him they were family, just a different kind of family.

They are sold at a young age by the Thenardiers to a fellow member of the criminal fraternity who can make use of them. As that use involves the extortion of money to pay for their upkeep, they enter a pampered existence infinitely better than they had previously known. All is well until their cozy existence is brought to an end. Their 'mother', with whom they live alone, is arrested by the police. The boys, who are playing outside, return home to find the house locked. They have been left a note that contains directions on where to go but it blows away in the wind. They are marooned, out on the streets in the middle of winter, with no knowledge of what to do and nobody to watch out for them. It is in this state that Gavroche finds them. Gavroche spends one night with them and tells them to return the following day if they need to but he never sees them again.

We meet them one more time, a few weeks later, wandering in the Luxembourg gardens:

> *The two little abandoned creatures had arrived in the vicinity of the grand fountain, and, rather bewildered by all this light, they tried to hide themselves, the instinct of the poor and the weak in the presence of even impersonal magnificence; and they kept behind the swans' hutch. ... The little one repeated from time to time: "I am hungry." ... Almost at the same instant with the children, another couple approached the great basin. They consisted of a gentleman,*

*about fifty years of age, who was leading by the hand a little fellow of six. No doubt, a father and his son. The little man of six had a big brioche.*

*All at once, he caught sight of the two little ragged boys behind the green swan-hutch. "There is the beginning," said he. And, after a pause, he added: "Anarchy is entering this garden." In the meanwhile, his son took a bite of his brioche, spat it out and suddenly burst out crying. "What are you crying about?" demanded his father. "I am not hungry anymore," said the child. The father's smile became more accentuated. "One does not need to be hungry in order to eat a cake." "My cake tires me. It is stale." "Don't you want any more of it?" "No." The father pointed to the swans." Throw it to those web-footed friends." The child hesitated. A person may not want any more of his cake; but that is no reason for giving it away. The father went on: "Be humane. You must have compassion on animals." And, taking the cake from his son, he flung it into the basin. ... Father and son entered the labyrinth of walks which leads to the grand flight of steps near the clump of trees on the side of the Rue Madame. As soon as they had disappeared from view, the elder child hastily flung himself flat on his stomach on the rounding curb of the basin, and clinging to it with his left hand, and leaning over the water, on the verge of falling in, he stretched out his right hand with his stick towards the cake. ... Just as the swans came up, the stick touched the cake. The child gave it a brisk rap, drew in the brioche, frightened away the swans, seized the cake, and sprang to his feet. The cake was wet; but they were hungry and thirsty. The elder broke the cake into two portions, a large one and a small one, took the small one for himself, gave the large one to his brother, and said to him: "Ram that into your muzzle."*

Most of us like a happy ending and, if we can't have a happy ending, then we at least like to have a proper ending with all of the ends tied up. We feel cheated if we see a film or read a book where things are left incomplete. That is just what we are left with here. Everybody else's fate or future is secured but two small boys – five and seven – are left helplessly wandering. They, like Lazarus, crave the food that falls from the mouths of those with plenty yet, despite their obvious need, they too are disdainfully ignored.

Why are they left unresolved? Does Victor Hugo forget that he has created them? No! They serve to remind us that there is a world out there which is not pretty and is not joined up neatly. It's a world where children are lost and hungry and suffering.

Those of us living comfortably in the developed world will probably pass each day without seeing a homeless person. It is easy to bury our heads in the sand and forget that they exist but here are some sobering statistics. Around the world there are between 100 and 150 million street children. It has been said that if the human race were reduced to a group of ten children around a table:

- 3 will have plates heaped so high that they will never finish what is there.

- 2 will just about manage to live by scavenging what is discarded by the three.

- 3 will be permanently hungry

- 2 will soon be dead, one from dysentery and one from pneumonia.
(Source: www.abaana.org)

The Thenardier children live on in every continent and, thanks to modern telecommunication, in every home. The only excuse we can possibly have for not seeing them is the excuse of having our eyes closed. That, says Jesus, is no excuse at all.

Those children live on and are our responsibility just as surely

as Lazarus was the responsibility of Dives. As Gavroche prophet-
ically recognized them as his brothers so we need to realize that
they are our brothers too.

# Week 4 – Day 7

Questions for personal reflection or group discussion

Keyword for the week: Compassion

## Setting the scene
Watch the DVD (14 minutes)
Start: Scene 7 Cosette sweeping (43:25)
Finish: "I'll be father and mother to you" (55:15)
Start: Scene 10 Paris street scene (1:03:58)
Finish: "Vive La France" (1:05:55)

## i 2 i
*Issues to explore*
What stood out for you from this week's readings or movie clips?
Was there anything you didn't understand?
*Irritants*
Was there anything in the material with which you disagreed?

## The Day 6 Dilemma
The struggle that comes from being a person created in the image of God

How were the two boys in the Luxembourg gardens viewed? Do you see people living homeless or in poverty as a need or a problem? How might God wish us to respond differently?
How do you respond to the Eponines of this world?
How do you respond to the Gavroches of this world?
How do you respond to the Cosettes of this world?

## Living it out

*Be joyful in hope, patient in affliction, faithful in prayer. Share with the Lord's people who are in need. Practice hospitality. (Romans 12:12-13)*

Why do you think that many of the most joyful, patient, prayerful Christians are among the world's poorest people?

Who do you think that Paul is referring to by the phrase 'God's people'? Do you think that this in any way limits our responsibility to the wider world? Why not?

What do you understand by the phrase 'Practice hospitality'?

### i 2 i

*Insights*

What insights have you gained from this week's material?

*Implementation*

Did you resolve to change anything in your life? What steps do you need to take to achieve this?

# 5

# Fellowship

*That's why we get on well together, my coat and I. It has acquired all my folds, it does not bind me anywhere, it is molded on my deformities, it falls in with all my movements, I am only conscious of it because it keeps me warm. Old coats are just like old friends.*

# Week 5 – Day I

*Read Luke 15:11-13*

The French Revolution of 1789 overthrew the reigning Bourbon king Louis XVI and established a republic. This held until the dynamic leader of the army, Napoleon Bonaparte, staged a coup in 1797, going on to declare himself emperor in 1804. Bonaparte and France were opposed by various coalitions of European states until France was defeated in 1814 and Napoleon forced to abdicate. The Bourbon monarchy was restored under Louis XVIII, apart from a brief 100-day period in 1815. Napoleon, with 600 men, escaped from exile on the island of Elba and, returning to France, received overwhelming public support as he marched on Paris. Louis XVIII fled and Napoleon again briefly took control before being finally defeated at the battle of Waterloo. Napoleon was forced to abdicate for a second time. The remnants of the French army, now camped around Paris to protect the city, were ordered to surrender without a fight, an order which, although obeyed, was extremely unpopular. All officers of the Imperial Guard, whom the monarchy looked upon with deep suspicion, were banished from Paris; retired on pensions of half-pay and forced to live in designated places where they could be kept under constant surveillance. No honors awarded during the hundred days were recognized. They were nicknamed 'the brigands of the Loire'.

One such officer was Georges Pontmercy. He had fought under the republican government and under Napoleon.

*He accompanied Napoleon to the Island of Elba. At Waterloo, he was chief of a squadron of cuirassiers, in Dubois' brigade. It was he who captured the standard of the Lunenburg battalion. He came and cast the flag at the Emperor's feet. He was covered with blood. While tearing down the banner he had received a sword-cut across his face.*

*The Emperor, greatly pleased, shouted to him: "You are a colonel, you are a baron, you are an officer of the Legion of Honor!" Pontmercy replied: "Sire, I thank you for my widow."*

Mention has already been made of Thenardier fighting at Waterloo. This was almost certainly a fiction. Thenardier had indeed been at Waterloo but was more interested in plundering from the dead. By chance, he happened to steal from a soldier who was still alive. Equally by chance, the soldier regained consciousness at that very moment and mistakenly assumed that Thenardier had saved him from death. This was the scene depicted on Thenardier's badly painted inn sign. The soldier was Georges Pontmercy. After Waterloo he became one of the 'brigands of the Loire' and was retired to Vernon.

Prior to Waterloo, Georges had married and had a son, Marius but, sadly, his wife had died in that same year of 1815. His father-in-law, M. Gillenormand, who lives with an unmarried daughter, has very definite political views. These are royalist and they are ultra-royalist. To the old man, anyone who has fought under Napoleon is anathema.

After his daughter's death it is threatened that the child will be disinherited if he continues to live with Pontmercy. Marius is the closest blood relative and heir. The only alternative is for him to stay in poverty with his father and so he is reluctantly given up to his grandfather and aunt.

An agreement is signed forbidding Pontmercy from having any contact with his son on pain of disinheritance. Twice a year, Marius is allowed to write to his father under the dictation of his aunt. This is all that his grandfather will allow. Georges sends long, affectionate letters to his son in return but these are crumpled and thrown away. Around the house, Pontmercy is referred to as 'that brigand'. Thus, Marius grows up thinking that his father does not care for him and that he is a dishonorable scoundrel.

His father sticks to the agreement with one exception. Every two to three months he attends the same church service as Marius and watches unnoticed from behind a pillar at the back of the church.

Jesus told a story about a man with two sons. One day, the younger son came to him and asked for his share of the estate. On the basis that the firstborn son is given a double share (Deuteronomy 21), this would have amounted to a third of his father's assets.

- It is uncertain whether his request was lawful but it was certainly unusual and most definitely disrespectful. It was the same as saying to his father, "I wish you were dead". This was a young man who cared little for family relationships.

- This is confirmed in the following verse when the father does divide his assets between them. The word translated as property is the Greek word βίος (bios) which literally means life. He was giving the substance of his life to them.

- The son departs for a distant country. He has no need of his family now that he has got what he wanted.

- His actions in the distant country reveal that he was not interested in the money itself. He wasn't looking to invest or accumulate. He only wanted the money for the pleasure it could bring him.

- His selfish motives lead to him squandering his wealth.

The octogenarian Gillenormand is an unlikely candidate for the role of younger son but this is just how he behaves. He demands and gets Marius, the one thing of value left in his son-in-law's life.

His political leanings outweigh any family loyalties and the agreement severs all family ties. Does he have any interest in Marius himself? It's a difficult question to answer. He does love him in his own peculiar way but for now it can also be said that his chief concern is to make sure he is indoctrinated with the right political views. As we shall see later, this will ultimately lead to a squandering of their relationship.

Consider your relationships, whether they be within your family, friends, work, church or wherever. Ask yourself whether these are genuine friendships or whether your real motive has been to use other people for your own ends. You may find that you end up getting what you want but squandering what you really need.

# Week 5 – Day 2

*Read Luke 2:41-52*

As we saw yesterday, Marius grows up in an ultra-royalist household and, as is common for a child, he accepts these views without question. His grandfather dotes upon him but is one of those men who has trouble expressing his feelings and can often convey the opposite to what he intends:

> *There was also in this house, between this elderly spinster and this old man, a child, a little boy, who was always trembling and mute in the presence of M. Gillenormand. M. Gillenormand never addressed this child except in a severe voice, and sometimes, with uplifted cane: "Here, sir! rascal, scoundrel, come here! Answer me, you scamp! Just let me see you, you good-for-nothing!" etc., etc. He idolized him.*

In 1827, at the age of seventeen, Marius returns home one day to be told that he must go to visit his father at Vernon. His father is dying. Neither Marius nor his grandfather treat the matter with the highest priority. He could have got a coach that evening but does not travel until the following day and arrives at Vernon in the afternoon. He is too late. His father has just died. Among his few possessions is a message for Marius.

> *"For my son. The Emperor made me a Baron on the battlefield of Waterloo. Since the Restoration disputes my right to this title which I purchased with my blood, my son shall take it and bear it. That he will be worthy of it is a matter of course."* Below, the colonel had added:
> *"At that same battle of Waterloo, a sergeant saved my life. The man's name was Thenardier. I think that he has recently been keeping a little inn, in a village in the neighborhood of Paris, at Chelles or Montfermeil. If my son meets him, he will do all the good he can to Thenardier."*

Marius pockets the note, stays on for the funeral but thinks no more about it until one day, in church, he absent-mindedly sits in a seat reserved for the churchwarden, M. Mabeuf. He is asked to move but afterwards, the churchwarden searches him out and explains why he sits in that seat:

> *"It is from this place, that I have watched a poor, brave father come regularly, every two or three months, for the last ten years, since he had no other opportunity and no other way of seeing his child, because he was prevented by family arrangements.*
>
> *He came at the hour when he knew that his son would be brought to mass. The little one never suspected that his father was there. Perhaps he did not even know that he had a father, poor innocent! The father kept behind a pillar, so that he might not be seen. He gazed at his child and he wept. He adored that little fellow, poor man! I could see that. This spot has become sanctified in my sight, and I have contracted a habit of coming hither to listen to the mass. I prefer it to the stall to which I have a right, in my capacity of warden. I knew that unhappy gentleman a little, too. He had a father-in-law, a wealthy aunt, relatives, I don't know exactly what all, who threatened to disinherit the child if he, the father, saw him. He sacrificed himself in order that his son might be rich and happy some day. He was separated from him because of political opinions. Certainly, I approve of political opinions, but there are people who do not know where to stop. Mon Dieu! a man is not a monster because he was at Waterloo; a father is not separated from his child for such a reason as that. He was one of Bonaparte's colonels. He is dead, I believe. He lived at Vernon, where I have a brother who is a priest, and his name was something like Pontmarie or Montpercy. He had a fine sword-cut, on my honor."*
>
> *"Pontmercy," suggested Marius, turning pale.*

This leads to a complete change of Marius' mind. He researches his father's military history. He widens his political reading. He has cards printed which read, 'Le Baron Marius Pontmercy'. He becomes (in his words) a 'democratic Bonapartist'.

Jesus is twelve years old and has been to Jerusalem with his family and extended kith and kin. Unbeknown to his parents, he has stayed on in the Temple and is learning from and debating with the religious teachers. When they realize that he isn't with them they return to Jerusalem and retrieve him.

I don't want to suggest that Jesus was a rowdy adolescent but how typical is his response. They've been merrily doing their own thing. You've lost them. You're worried sick. And they can't see what all the fuss is about. It's all part of the transition to full independence. It goes along with pushing boundaries and developing their own view of the world.

This is a crucial phase in Jesus' moving from childhood to adulthood. In later Jewish custom, thirteen would mark the year of Bar Mitzvah and maturity. Jesus is still therefore a child but he is developing his own ideas and his own faith. He is keen to listen to the teachers and soak up all that he can. He asks questions and one presumes these are both to fill gaps in his knowledge and to challenge where necessary. Those with him are amazed at his level of understanding.

We need to recognize that, like Jesus, our faith and our spiritual understanding will always be developing. It is all part of the journey that we are on. Sometimes, as it was with Marius, we can move huge distances in very short spaces of time. We should expect every church to have people who are changing rapidly alongside people whose progress is more sedate. It may be people on fire with new-found faith. It may be people discovering charismatic experience. It may be people developing more conservative or more liberal standpoints.

The challenge as a church family is to recognize this and be flexible enough to contain it. Too much rigidity and we run the risk – as Gillenormand will discover – of splitting our family apart.

# Week 5 – Day 3

*Read Matthew 18:21-22*

Marius, as we have seen, has been baptized into a new political creed. He disappears from the family home for long periods. These trips are for three purposes. He travels to libraries to read up on French political history and his father's military career; he visit his father's grave and he searches for Thenardier of whom there is now no trace.

His grandfather and aunt assume that a girl must lie behind the absences. Therefore, when they find unguarded the medallion that Marius wears around his neck, they are unable to resist looking at its contents. They are devastated to find that it contains the message from Georges Pontmercy.

*A few moments later, Marius made his appearance. He entered. Even before he had crossed the threshold, he saw his grandfather holding one of his own cards in his hand, and on catching sight of him, the latter exclaimed with his air of bourgeois and grinning superiority which was something crushing: "Well! Well! Well! Well! Well! So you are a baron now. I present you my compliments. What is the meaning of this?" Marius reddened slightly and replied: "It means that I am the son of my father." M. Gillenormand ceased to laugh, and said harshly: "I am your father."*

*"My father," retorted Marius, with downcast eyes and a severe air, "was a humble and heroic man, who served the Republic and France gloriously, who was great in the greatest history that men have ever made, who lived in the bivouac for a quarter of a century, beneath grape-shot and bullets, in snow and mud by day, beneath rain at night, who captured two flags, who received twenty wounds, who died forgotten and abandoned, and who never committed but one mistake, which was to love too fondly two ingrates, his country and myself."*

The result of the argument is that Marius is ordered out of the house, a departure he is all too happy to make. The rift is exacerbated by the loss of the message.

*While carrying Marius' "duds" precipitately to his chamber, at his grandfather's command, Nicolette [the maid] had, inadvertently, let fall, probably, on the attic staircase, which was dark, that medallion of black shagreen which contained the paper penned by the colonel. Neither paper nor case could afterwards be found. Marius was convinced that "Monsieur Gillenormand" – from that day forth he never alluded to him otherwise – had flung "his father's testament" in the fire. He knew by heart the few lines which the colonel had written, and, consequently, nothing was lost. But the paper, the writing, that sacred relic, all that was his very heart. What had been done with it?*

It will be four years before Marius and his grandfather meet again.

Marius continues his law studies and learns English and German in order to do translation work to make ends meet. He is permanently dressed in black as a sign of mourning for his father. He rents a cheap room in the same dilapidated building that Valjean and Cosette had stayed in briefly on their arrival in Paris, and tries to live as economically as possible. His clothes are perpetually on the point of being worn out and he can make a lamb chop last three days – 'On the first day he ate the meat, on the second he ate the fat, on the third he gnawed the bone.' This is a poverty of his own choosing, as his scruples will not allow him either to live on credit or to accept the sums of money sent to him by his aunt.

Marius is smarting. He is offended on two counts. Firstly, for himself and the rejection of his new ideology but perhaps, more so, for what he sees as the slight to his dead father. In such circumstances, it is easy for misunderstandings and suspicions to occur and he is now also convinced that his grandfather has deliberately destroyed the one personal memento that he has been left. He is, therefore, determined that he will have no contact with his family and will live in separation and poverty as a point of principle.

When we feel unfairly treated as Marius did, then bitterness can easily creep in. Our natural instinct is to hold on to the hurt and to hit back as much as we can. In Christian terms, though, forgiveness is a key weapon. We need to understand that forgiveness is not so much about letting others off the hook as it is about neutralizing the bitterness within us.

At the beginning of Genesis is a story that is usually overlooked. Cain kills Abel and is banished. God places a mark upon Cain and proclaims that if anyone kills him they will be avenged seven times. Lamech is the great-great-great grandson of Cain. One day, Lamech returns home and tells his wives that he has killed a man in self-defense. Fearing that he might be the victim of an unmerited revenge attack, he says to them:

*"Adah and Zillah, listen to me; wives of Lamech, hear my words. I have killed a man for wounding me, a young man for injuring me. If Cain is avenged seven times, then Lamech seventy-seven times."* (Genesis 4:23-24)

The word translated as either seventy-seven or seventy-times-seven (both here and in today's reading) is really a figure of speech. It is used to symbolize an inexpressibly large number. In other words, Lamech is voicing that desire within each of us that wants to keep on hurting and hurting and hurting the person we feel has unfairly wronged us.

When Jesus replies to Peter's question about forgiveness, he is drawing on this same story but it is turned around. If the human way is to go on avenging then the Christian way must be to keep on forgiving. We forgive without limit. It is only through such actions that the chains of bitterness can be broken and human relationships can hope to be restored.

# Week 5 – Day 4

*Read Matthew 10:1-4*

When Marius left his grandfather's house he had precisely thirty francs together with his watch and a bag containing some clothes. By chance, he meets a fellow law student Lesgle who introduces him to another student, Courfeyrac. Courfeyrac takes Marius under his wing and they become the best of friends.

Marius is introduced to the ABC society. These are young people with strong republican leanings. The name ABC is a play on words. It refers to their cover activity of educating children but also represents the French word 'abaissé' meaning 'the underdog' or 'the people'.

*The Friends of the A B C were not numerous, it was a secret society in the state of embryo, we might almost say a clique, if cliques give rise to heroes. They assembled in Paris in two localities, near the fish market, in a wine shop called Corinthe, of which more will be heard later on, and near the Pantheon in a little café in the Rue Saint-Michel called the Cafe Musain, now torn down; the first of these meeting places was close to the workingman, the second to the students.*

*The meetings of the Friends of the A B C were usually held in a back room of the Cafe Musain. ... There they conversed in very loud tones about everything, and in whispers of other things. An old map of France under the Republic was nailed to the wall – a sign quite sufficient to excite the suspicion of a police agent.*

Each of the significant members is described in turn.

**Enjolras:** The leader; an only son of wealthy parents; angelically good looking. Charming; both scholarly and warlike; a thinker and a man of action; youthful – *Grown to manhood he still appeared* *a youth, his twenty-two years seeming no more than seventeen;* wedded to idealistic philosophy rather than sexuality – *it did not seem as though he were aware there was on earth a thing called woman. He had but one passion – the right; but one thought – to overthrow the obstacle.*

**Combeferre**: Pragmatist; gentle; wise; scholarly; precise; eclectic; persuader. He and Enjolras go together. If Enjolras is the irrefutable logic of revolution then Combeferre is its philosophy:

> *It is not that Combeferre was not capable of fighting, he did not refuse a hand-to-hand combat with the obstacle, and to attack it by main force and explosively; but it suited him better to bring the human race into accord with its destiny gradually, by means of education, the inculcation of axioms, the promulgation of positive laws; and, between two lights, his preference was rather for illumination than for conflagration. A bonfire will create a glow, no doubt, but why not await the dawn?*

**Jean Prouvaire**: Soft-hearted; loving; kind; erudite; romantic; meditative – *There were two sides to his mind, the side of men and the side of God;* shy; fearless.

**Feuilly**: Orphan; working man; fan-maker earning three francs a day; self-educated; reads in order to be better informed; warm-hearted; affectionate.

**Courfeyrac**: Marius' new friend; full of youthful ardor – *Enjolras was the leader, Combeferre was the guide, Courfeyrac was the center. The others gave more light, he shed more warmth; the truth is, that he possessed all the qualities of a center, roundness and radiance.*

**Bahorel**: Born agitator; bold; generous; courageous; spendthrift; a link to other groups; *loving nothing so much as a quarrel, unless it* *were an uprising; and nothing so much as an uprising, unless it were a revolution; always ready to smash a windowpane, then to tear up the pavement, then to demolish a government, just to see the effect of it.*

**Lesgle**: Cheerful; one who succeeds at nothing but laughs at everything; extravagant when he has money.

**Joly**: Hypochondriac; joyful (when not imaging himself ill); eccentric.

**Grantaire**: Boxer; gymnast; dancer; drinker; skeptic with little interest in revolution. He is there because he is devoted to Enjolras.

*All these young men, so diverse but who, when all is said, deserved to be taken seriously, had a religion in common: Progress. All were the direct descendants of the French Revolution, and even the most frivolous became serious at the mention of 1789. ... They stood, without having passed through any intermediary stages, for uncompromising right and absolute duty. United and initiated, they were the underground portrayal of the ideal.*

It can be a little confusing reading the accounts of the ABC society. Each of the characters is given a lengthy introduction but an underdeveloped personality. With one or two exceptions, the impression is given that nobody would notice if their speeches were swapped around. And that is entirely the point. In life these may be diverse characters but in politics they are one beast with many heads.

When Jesus called the twelve disciples he was selecting a diverse and potentially volatile cast of characters. There were enough egos present to spark regular squabbles about status. There was James and John, the 'Sons of Thunder'; there was a zealot (an advocate of armed revolution) and a tax-collector; and a whole lot more all rubbing together. What was it that united them? They were united by faith in Jesus but also by the mission and ministry to which he called them. He sent them out and gave them the authority to exorcize demons and heal the sick. Later, after Jesus' death and resurrection, their fellowship would be further built up by the Holy Spirit.

The disciples stand for all that the church is today. Take any church and you should find a hugely disparate collection of people. They will come from many backgrounds and many viewpoints. Most will probably only have the church as a common meeting point. Some will be so different that, in another context, squabbles could easily arise. What binds us together, like the students, is a common vision. That vision comes from the Jesus who calls us, empowers us and unites us through the Holy Spirit.

The word 'division' derives from the Latin prefix meaning 'apart' and the verb *videre*, to see. Its root derivation therefore comes from seeing things differently. We shall see tomorrow that Marius separates from the students because he does not share their political vision and sees things differently to them. If we are to hold together as a church then we must ensure that we all share the same God-given vision. That will still leave plenty of room for discussion (and disagreement!) about details but the central, driving vision is crucial. Without it we lose our unity. Or as somebody has famously put it, Vision + Vision = Division.

# Week 5 – Day 5

*Read Matthew 19:1-6*

Marius ceases to meet with the ABC students. He realizes that they share different political views to him but it is also that his political ardor is cooling:

*All passions except those of the heart are dissipated by reverie. Marius' political fevers vanished thus. The Revolution of 1830 assisted in the process, by satisfying and calming him. He remained the same, setting aside his fits of wrath. He still held the same opinions. Only, they had been tempered. To speak accurately, he had no longer any opinions, he had sympathies.*

A further reason is that Marius becomes engrossed in falling in love. His life of poverty means that he takes long walks as these are free and fill up time. He walks in the Luxembourg gardens. There, on a bench, he often notices an old man talking to what he presumes is his teenage daughter. There is nothing remarkable about them. The girl is thirteen or fourteen, awkward and 'almost ugly'. Marius simply notes their presence and move on.

For several months, at the beginning of 1831, Marius doesn't visit the garden. On his return he finds that a transformation has taken place:

*The person whom he now beheld was a tall and beautiful creature, possessed of all the most charming lines of a woman at the precise moment when they are still combined with all the most ingenuous graces of the child; a pure and fugitive moment, which can be expressed only by these two words, "fifteen years." She had wonderful brown hair, shaded with threads of gold, a brow that seemed made of marble, cheeks that seemed made of rose leaf, a pale flush, an agitated whiteness, an exquisite mouth, whence smiles darted like sunbeams, and words like music, a head such as Raphael would have given to Mary, set upon a neck that Jean Goujon would have attributed to a Venus. And, in order that nothing might be lacking to this bewitching face, her nose was not handsome, it was pretty; neither straight nor curved, neither Italian nor Greek; it was the Parisian nose, that is to say, spiritual, delicate, irregular, pure, which drives painters to despair, and charms poets.*

It takes a few weeks but then:

*One day, the air was warm, the Luxembourg was inundated with light and shade, the sky was as pure as though the angels had washed it that morning, the sparrows were giving vent to little twitters in the depths of the chestnut trees. Marius had thrown open his whole soul to nature, he was not thinking of anything, he simply lived and breathed, he passed near the bench, the young girl raised her eyes to him, the two glances met. What was there in the young girl's glance on this occasion? Marius could not have told. There was nothing and there was everything. A spark had passed between them.*

Marius is obsessed. He visits the gardens every day and secret glances pass between them, of which the father is unaware. On one occasion Marius follows them to their home and questions the porter. They disappear. For the girl is Cosette and Valjean is forever on his guard.

It may seem ridiculous to say that a couple is in love having done no more than exchange a few glances but that's exactly how Victor Hugo plays it.

*The glance has been so much abused in love romances that it has finally fallen into disrepute. One hardly dares to say, nowadays, that two beings fell in love because they looked at each other. That is the way people do fall in love, nevertheless, and the only way. The rest*

*is nothing, but the rest comes afterwards. Nothing is more real than*
*these great shocks which two souls convey to each other by the*
*exchange of that spark.*

And modern psychology is on Hugo's side. First impressions and physical attraction play a more than significant role in most relationships and provide a potential pitfall for the single Christian. It is easy to form a relationship first and ask questions about the deeper things of life afterwards. If we do find differences on matters of faith, we can convince ourselves that these don't really matter or will work out over time.

When I was in my early twenties, I pastored a church youth group. On one occasion, one of the girls asked me whether she should go out with a particular boy. The question was prompted by the fact that she was a Christian and he wasn't. He seemed nice enough so, having given her all the appropriate guidance, I left it up to her. As it turned out they did go out together and he ended up becoming a Christian.

If I were asked the same question today I would give a different answer. It's not that I have become more hardline per se but over years of ministry I have seen so many people (mostly women) whose Christian walk has been restricted through having a non-Christian partner.

The word cleave is one of those wonderful words that has meanings which are the opposite of each other. Thus it can mean both to join together and to split apart. Its history is of two slightly different Anglo-Saxon verbs that merged together in the Middle Ages. From the two roots we get cleavage (joining together) and cleaver (splitting apart).

The word is used in the King James translation of today's reading where Jesus speaks about a man leaving his parents and cleaving to a wife so that the two become 'one flesh'. He makes clear that he sees this as being a lifelong commitment of love and loyalty. The word is also used in Acts 11 where Barnabas encourages the believers to cleave to God. This too is a lifelong commitment.

It doesn't take a genius to work out that problems will occur when these two relationships come into conflict. If our partner does not share our faith then, however sympathetic they may appear, there will be an inevitable pulling in different directions. Cleaving to one will mean being cleaved from the other.

# Week 5 – Day 6

*Read Mark 3:31-35*

It is during the summer of 1831 that Marius falls in love with Cosette and then loses contact with her. In this same period, he becomes aware that his neighbors, the Jondrette family, are due to be evicted. Anonymously, he settles the debt for them.

The following February, he meets and talks to the older Jondrette daughter. The Jondrettes are in fact the Thenardiers living under one of many aliases and the girl is Eponine. Marius is appalled by her tales of poverty and, discovering a peephole in the wall between them, peers into their squalor:

> *Marius was poor, and his chamber was poverty-stricken, but as his poverty was noble, his garret was neat. The den upon which his eye now rested was abject, dirty, fetid, pestiferous, mean, sordid. The only furniture consisted of a straw chair, an infirm table, some old bits of crockery, and in two of the corners, two indescribable pallets; all the light was furnished by a dormer window of four panes, draped with spiders' webs. Through this aperture there penetrated just enough light to make the face of a man appear like the face of a phantom.*

As Marius watches, the Thenardiers are visited by Valjean and Cosette. Valjean has been a recipient of one of Thenardier's begging letters and comes bearing money, clothes and blankets. Thenardier pleads (exaggerated) rent arrears and Valjean promises to return later that evening with the amount needed. Valjean does not recognize Thenardier but Thenardier recognizes him.

After Valjean and Cosette leave, the Thenardiers make plans to capture Valjean on his return. They will then kidnap Cosette and demand 200,000 francs for her safe return.

Marius is still watching and he is horrified. He rushes to the police station and reports the matter to the Inspector on duty. It is Javert! Javert gives Marius two pistols and tells him to return to his room and keep watch. The police will be waiting nearby. Marius is to fire a pistol at the appropriate moment and this will be the sign for the police to pounce.

Marius also realizes that Eponine has a great familiarity with Paris and asks her to track down Cosette's address for him. He is oblivious to the fact that Eponine herself has feelings for him.

At six o'clock, everything is ready. Thenardier is waiting with the criminal gang, Patron-Minette. Marius is watching. Valjean returns. The criminals have a rope ladder hanging from the window should a quick escape become necessary. Valjean is about to be captured and Marius is about to fire his pistol when Thenardier reveals his true identity:

*Marius did not hear this reply. Anyone who had seen him at that moment through the darkness would have perceived that he was haggard, stupid, thunder-struck. At the moment when Jondrette said: "My name is Thenardier," Marius had trembled in every limb, and had leaned against the wall, as though he felt the cold of a steel blade through his heart. ... Let the reader recall what that name meant to him! That name he had worn on his heart, inscribed in his father's testament! He bore it at the bottom of his mind, in the depths of his memory, in that sacred injunction: "A certain Thenardier saved my life. If my son encounters him, he will do him all the good that lies in his power." That name, it will be remembered, was one of the pieties of his soul; he mingled it with the name of his father in his worship. What! This man was that Thenardier, that innkeeper of Montfermeil whom he had so long and so vainly sought! He had found him at last, and how? His father's savior was a ruffian!*

Marius is paralyzed and can do nothing. He is torn between love for his father and his love for Cosette. His father's dying wish had been that he search for Thenardier and reward him. He knows that if he shoots his pistol and Thenardier is arrested it will mean a long jail term or possible death sentence. Not quite the reward that his father had in mind! But, if he does nothing it could lead to Cosette being harmed. What would you do?

Thankfully for Marius, his role in the drama does not turn out to be vital. Despite the absence of a gunshot, Javert acts and storms the room. The Thenardiers and their accomplices are arrested. The only person to make use of the rope ladder to escape is Valjean.

The gospels make clear that, in the early days of Jesus' ministry, his family did not support him, did not believe in him (John 7) and even thought him mad. Later this would change and Jesus' brother James was a leader of the early Church in Jerusalem. At this moment, however, Mark reports that his family are looking to 'take charge' of him which presumably means forcible restraint and removal.

Jesus' response? He asks the question of those present, "Who are my mother and my brothers?" and then adds that anyone who does God's will is his 'brother and sister and mother'. It goes alongside other seemingly harsh comments that Jesus makes about family. Jesus is critical in response to a would-be follower who wants to say goodbye to his family (Luke 9) and elsewhere says that anyone who does not hate his family – father, mother, wife, children, brothers, sisters – cannot be his disciple (Luke 14).

How should we read these comments? Certainly not literally because elsewhere in the Gospels it is implied that Jesus took his family responsibilities very seriously. Rather, Jesus is making use of hyperbole to make a point. We are not meant to hate our families but to recognize the fact that there may be a conflict between family demands and God's demands. Jesus is pressing the point that in such a conflict, God must be the winner.

It's a tough call, as Marius discovered. Family loyalties can run very deep, particularly when we are emotionally bound to the dead, but they must not be allowed to deflect us from the right course of action.

# Week 5 – Day 7

Questions for personal reflection or group discussion

Keyword for the week: Fellowship

**Setting the scene**
Watch the DVD (13 minutes)
Start: Scene 9 The North Gate of Paris (58:12)
Finish: "Clear this garbage off the street" (1:11:18)

**i 2 i**
*Issues to explore*
What stood out for you from this week's readings or movie clip?
Was there anything you didn't understand?
*Irritants*
Was there anything in the material with which you disagreed?

**The Day 6 Dilemma**
The struggle that comes from being a person created in the image of God

What was the dilemma that Marius faced?
What might you have done in the circumstances? Why?
In many cases people act as they think somebody else would want. What additional problems can arise when that person is dead?

**Living it out**

*For by the grace given me I say to every one of you: Do not think of yourself more highly than you ought, but rather think of yourself with sober judgment, in accordance with the faith God has distributed to each of you. For just as each of us has one body with*

*many members, and these members do not all have the same
function, so in Christ we, though many, form one body, and each
member belongs to all the others. ... Love must be sincere. Hate what
is evil; cling to what is good. Be devoted to one another in love.
Honor one another above yourselves. Never be lacking in zeal, but
keep your spiritual fervor, serving the Lord. Be joyful in hope,
patient in affliction, faithful in prayer. Share with the Lord's people
who are in need. Practice hospitality. (Romans 12:3-5 and 9-13)*

*"For by the grace given me I say to every one of you:"* How does the
idea of grace help us to see other people differently?

In what ways are humility and forgiveness the keys to a
healthy church?

How can increasing zeal and spiritual fervor threaten the
harmony of a church? How do we overcome that threat?

And how might we encourage those who have to balance
spiritual fervor with non-Christian partners?

**i 2 i**
*Insights*
What insights have you gained from this week's material?
*Implementation*
Did you resolve to change anything in your life? What steps do
you need to take to achieve this?

# 6

# Darkness

*The pupil dilates in darkness and in the end finds light, just as the soul dilates in misfortune and in the end finds God.*

## Week 6 – Day 1

*Read Luke 13:1-5*

The events of the next few days will be played out under cover of darkness, either above ground or underground. Neither is the darkness solely external. Our characters are undergoing the kind of internal darkness that all of us have to endure from time to time.

On June 5 1832, four months after Marius' dilemma and the arrest of Patron-Minette, there is fighting and barricades on the streets of Paris. Before we follow our cast to the barricades, it is time to meet again an old acquaintance.

You will recall that Mabeuf was the elderly church warden who had, unwittingly, revealed to Marius the secrets of his family. By 1832, he is eighty years old. He is an academic whose chief interest is in botany. He had published a work entitled, 'Flora of the Environs of Cauteretz', which gives him a steady if unspectacular income and enables him both to live humbly with a housekeeper and build up a library.

He is as disinterested in politics as he is interested in plants:

*All political opinions were matters of indifference to him, and he approved them all, without distinction, provided they left him in peace ... M. Mabeuf's political opinion consisted in a passionate love for plants, and, above all, for books. ... He did not understand how men could busy themselves with hating each other because of silly stuff like the charter, democracy, legitimacy, monarchy, the republic, etc., when there were in the world all sorts of mosses, grasses, and shrubs which they might be looking at, and heaps of folios ... which they might turn over.*

One might be tempted to see *Les Misérables* as a kind of morality tale. Man of faith (Valjean) rises from pile due to good behavior

134

and discipline whilst bad behavior (the Thenardiers) or bad choices (Fantine) sink you to the bottom. Mabeuf is the exception that pricks this over-neat bubble. He is pushed to the depths of poverty through no fault of his own and confirms Victor Hugo's assertion that *les misérables* consist of both the infamous and the unfortunate.

Firstly, a notary's negligence deprives him of a vital 10,000 francs. At roughly the same time, the July Revolution of 1830 and the uncertainty that follows have a devastating effect on the publishing trade. Nobody wants to buy his book and, when he is reduced to selling his library of books and prints in order to survive, he receives a pittance for them.

He is descending into the darkness and it is no coincidence that in his final days, three significant events occur at night. It is Mabeuf to whom Eponine mysteriously appears one evening (like a grotesque goblin) to water his plants. Then Gavroche, aware of Mabeuf's situation, picks the pocket of a member of Patron-Minette and tosses a purse containing over 120 francs into his garden. Unfortunately, Mabeuf is too honest to do other than hand the purse in to the police where it is never claimed. Finally, there appears some hope from the involvement of a Government minister.

*He belonged to the Horticultural Society. His destitution became known there. The president of the society came to see him, promised to speak to the Minister of Agriculture and Commerce about him, and did so. "Why, what!" exclaimed the Minister, "I should think so! An old savant! A botanist! An inoffensive man! Something must be done for him!" On the following day, M. Mabeuf received an invitation to dine with the Minister. Trembling with joy, he showed the letter to Mother Plutarque* [his housekeeper]. *"We are saved!" said he.*

*On the day appointed, he went to the Minister's house. He perceived that his ragged cravat, his long, square coat, and his waxed shoes astonished the ushers. No one spoke to him, not even the Minister. About ten o'clock in the evening, while he was still waiting for a word, he heard the Minister's wife, a beautiful woman in a low-necked gown whom he had not ventured to approach, inquire: "Who is that old gentleman?" He returned home on foot at midnight, in a driving rainstorm.*

The carriage ride to the minister's house had cost him a book from his collection.

Jesus is asked to comment upon an incident in which Pontius Pilate had ordered the execution of some Galileans, who were in the middle of offering sacrifices in the Temple. The incident is not recorded outside of today's reading but fits with other events of Pilate's governorship. Neither do we know whether Jesus' informants were looking for a political or a philosophical response.

Jesus gives them the latter. Why had this happened? Did it mean that these Galileans were worse sinners than any other Galileans? Was this a kind of punishment for wickedness? Not according to Jesus.

Then he refers to a second tragedy, a natural disaster where eighteen people had been crushed by a water tower. Were these eighteen more sinful than the other inhabitants of Jerusalem? Not according to Jesus.

What Jesus is refuting here is some wrong-headed thinking that is given voice in the Old Testament and is still believed today. It begins with something that is generally true. If you set out to live a disciplined life and follow God's guidance then you should prosper. Conversely, if you live an ill-disciplined life and ignore God's guidance then you are less likely to prosper. Here, though, is where the dodgy logic comes in. People began looking at those who had failed or were sick and assumed that they must have done something wrong to bring it upon themselves. Read the book of Job if you want an extended study (and debunking!) of the theory.

Yet we do the same thing to ourselves today. A tragedy occurs – sickness, unemployment, the death of a loved one, a miscarriage etc. – and we are pitched into the darkness. How often then does the question form on our lips – "What have I done to deserve this?"

If you are presently battling the darkness let the words of Jesus be an answer for you. Like Mabeuf you have probably done nothing to deserve it but know that, as we shall see later in the week, Jesus goes through the darkness with you.

# Week 6 — Day 2

*Read Matthew 6:25-34*

The July Revolution of 1830 was a compromise. It exiled an unpopular king but maintained a monarchy albeit one surrounded by democratic mechanisms. That France had not returned to a republic was a grievance to some, particularly in the absence of any further constitutional reforms. For many of the agitators, therefore, the barricades of 1832 were a return to unfinished business.

First, though, we need to bring ourselves up to date.

February 3 1832:

- The attack on Valjean and the arrest of the Thenardiers and Patron-Minette.

- Marius moves out of his room to stay with his friend Courfeyrac.

April:

- Eponine takes Marius to Valjean and Cosette's house in the Rue Plumet.

- Marius makes contact with Cosette and they begin to meet secretly in the house's garden every evening.

April/May:

- Thenardier and Patron-Minette (except Madame Thenardier) escape from jail.

June 3:

- Valjean decides that Paris is no longer safe and that he and Cosette should go to England.

- Patron-Minette set out to burgle Valjean's house but are thwarted by Eponine.

- Cosette tells Marius that she will soon be leaving Paris. Marius scratches his address on her garden wall.

June 4:

- Marius visits his grandfather for the first time in four years and asks for financial assistance in marrying Cosette. His grandfather approves of the choice but suggests that he consider taking her as a mistress. Marius storms out at what he perceives as a fresh insult.

- Valjean becomes more concerned when he discovers the address on the wall and a note from Eponine telling them to clear out.

June 5:

- Valjean and Cosette move to their house in the Rue de l'Homme Arme.

- The funeral of General Lamarque is an agreed signal for rioting and barricades on the streets.

- Marius wakes just as Courfeyrac, Enjolras, Feuilly, and Combeferre are setting out. Courfeyrac asks him if he is going to the funeral. Marius has no idea of the significance of this question.

- In the evening Marius visits Cosette but finds the house deserted. He assumes she has left for England and abandoned him.

- Eponine is at the house and tells him that his friends are waiting for him at the barricade in the Rue de la Chanvrerie.

- In the Rue de l'Homme Arme, Valjean learns about the relationship between Cosette and Marius by accidentally reading the imprint of one of Cosette's letters left on her blotter.

The students of the ABC society are gathered at the barricade. So too are Eponine and Gavroche. One unexpected face is also there. Mabeuf, the man devoid of political opinion, has run out of food, money and books.

Why are people at the barricade?

- Eponine is there because she knows she has no prospect of winning Marius and hopes that she might at least die alongside him.

- Gavroche is there because he has a sense of natural justice and a liking for anything that gives the establishment a kick up the backside. Perhaps more sadly, his life is limited to an eternal present. He has no aspirations for the future and therefore isn't troubled by the prospect of that life being ended.

- Mabeuf on the other hand sees his life as already having come to an end. His actions are probably part suicide and part deathbed realization that the society that has wiped him out needs to be changed.

- Marius is on the way. He is pictured entering into a physical blackness as he gropes his way through the darkened streets but also a spiritual blackness. His presence isn't due to political ideology. His primary aim is to die. Despair has a lot to do with it, mingled with spite at the girlfriend and grandfather who (he believes) have rejected him. But, as he walks, he develops more glorious illusions of following in his father's footsteps:

*He said to himself that his day had also come now, that his hour had struck, that following his father, he too was about to show himself brave, intrepid, bold, to run to meet the bullets, to offer his breast to bayonets, to shed his blood, to seek the enemy, to seek death, that he was about to wage war in his turn and descend to the field of battle, and that the field of battle upon which he was to descend was the street, and that the war in which he was about to engage was civil war!*

- Why are the students there? You might think this the easiest question to answer. Surely they are there because they want to align society to their political views. The answer, however, is not as clear as you might imagine. For political activists they seem surprisingly naïve, with ideal-istic dreams of a utopian society but no clear idea of how to achieve it. We are also told very little about their political beliefs other than that they cherish the memory of the 1789 Revolution. This could put them into one of several quite distinct groupings. The reason is simple. They have been created in order to be killed. They have a death wish. Their precise political beliefs are unimportant. They represent a strand of the (then) contemporary young male psyche which thought it romantic to die in a noble cause. Thus, they persist at the barricade even when they know that it will achieve nothing.

A phrase often used of suicide victims is that they acted 'while the balance of their mind was disturbed'. What we have here is a collection of disturbed minds; of people who place no value on their future lives with most determined to throw those lives away. It can feel like that in the darkness. It doesn't seem that life is ever going to get any better.

Jesus paints a picture of a God who is there in every day with us. According to Jesus, God will provide for you just as surely as he feeds the birds and clothes the flowers. Even when the future seems bleak, remember that, with God around, miracles can and will happen. Life is precious. Don't be tempted to waste it.

# Week 6 – Day 3

*Read Luke 6:27-36*

Marius reaches the barricade and his arrival is timely. He still has the two pistols that Javert had given him for alerting the police during Thenardier's attempted kidnap of Valjean. Each has a single bullet. One bullet saves the life of Gavroche; one the life of Courfeyrac. The barricade is about to be overrun by soldiers. Not fearing for his own life, Marius ascends the barricade with a lighted torch and keg of gunpowder which he threatens to explode. The soldiers scatter and a reprieve of several hours is won.

A dying Eponine gives Marius a letter from Cosette which contains their new address. She had previously concealed it as part of her plan to lure Marius to the barricade. Marius, in turn, writes a final letter to Cosette which he sends via Gavroche, thinking that this will remove Gavroche from the carnage to come.

Marius' heroics mean that the rebels at the barricade look to him alongside Enjolras for guidance. Very soon he is put into an invidious position. It is agreed that men with wives and families should be sent home and not sacrificed. The easiest way to get away from the barricade is to dress in a soldier's uniform of which they have four and five possible candidates all of whom want to be the one to stay. Marius is asked to make the decision. At that point a fifth uniform, that of a National Guardsman, is thrown on to the pile. Valjean too has arrived at the barricade.

*The emotion aroused was indescribable. "Who is this man?" demanded Bossuet.*

*"He is a man who saves others," replied Combeferre.*

*Marius added in a grave voice: "I know him." This guarantee satisfied every one. Enjolras turned to Jean Valjean. "Welcome, citizen." And he added: "You know that we are about to die." Jean Valjean, without replying, helped the insurgent whom he was saving to don his uniform.*

Valjean proves invaluable. He is a crack marksman but always shoots at objects rather than people. At other times he tends to the injured.

Earlier in the evening, Gavroche had identified one of the men at the barricade as a police spy. It is Javert who has been tied up and promised that he will die at a later point. Valjean asks to be allowed to carry out the execution and takes him out of sight around the corner.

*Jean Valjean thrust the pistol under his arm and fixed on Javert a look which it required no words to interpret: "Javert, it is I."*

*Javert replied: "Take your revenge."*

*Jean Valjean drew from his pocket a knife, and opened it.*

*"A clasp-knife!" exclaimed Javert, "you are right. That suits you better."*

*Jean Valjean cut the martingale which Javert had about his neck, then he cut the cords on his wrists, then, stooping down, he cut the cord on his feet; and, straightening himself up, he said to him: "You are free."*

*Javert was not easily astonished. Still, master of himself though he was, he could not repress a start. He remained open-mouthed and motionless. Jean Valjean continued: "I do not think that I shall escape from this place. But if, by chance, I do, I live, under the name of Fauchelevent, in the Rue de l'Homme Arme, No. 7."*

*Javert snarled like a tiger, which made him half open one corner of his mouth, and he muttered between his teeth: "Take care."*

*"Go," said Jean Valjean.*

*Javert began again: "You said Fauchelevent, Rue de l'Homme Arme?"*

*"Number 7." Javert repeated in a low voice: "Number 7."*

*He buttoned up his coat once more, resumed the military stiffness between his shoulders, made a half turn, folded his arms and, supporting his chin on one of his hands, he set out in the direction of the Halles. Jean Valjean followed him with his eyes:*

*A few minutes later, Javert turned round and shouted to Jean Valjean: "You annoy me. Kill me, rather." ... "Be off with you," said Jean Valjean. Javert retreated slowly. A moment later he turned the corner of the Rue des Precheurs. When Javert had disappeared, Jean Valjean fired his pistol in the air. Then he returned to the barricade and said: "It is done."*

Today's reading comes from a time when Jesus was teaching a large crowd of his disciples. They might have been forgiven for getting up and going home, such is the difficulty of the demands. We are familiar with the Christian requirements for forgiveness and non-retaliation but here Jesus goes way, way beyond. Love your enemies. Do good to those who hurt you. Wish blessing upon those who curse you. Even pray for those who persecute you. It's tough with a capital T.

Where do we start? – Actually, with the last verse of the passage. We are asked to show mercy because God is that kind of a God and we are his children. Did Jesus pray forgiveness on those who crucified him on a cross? Yes he did. Does God go on loving and seeking to turn around even the worst sinners imaginable? Yes he does. We do it because God does it.

And we do it because it is the fastest way to make an impact on others. Jesus was building up his listeners to be a living, witnessing community in the world. What a difference it makes to our opponents when we not only fail to seek revenge but bring blessing instead. We don't see it yet but what a difference Valjean makes in the life of Javert.

Darkness brings with it added temptations. From the dawn of time, light has been synonymous with good and darkness with evil. It probably stems from the fact that people are more disposed to do evil things at night when their actions can't be seen. The same can be true of times of spiritual darkness too. The Devil will try to cloud your mind concerning values and beliefs you have always held dear. Do not listen. Stay close – as Valjean does – to the truths of the Bible. You may also be tempted to try to improve things by making major changes in your life. Again, do nothing unless you clearly hear the voice of God speaking to you, particularly where it concerns paths upon which you feel that God has previously set you.

Be patient. The light will come.

# Week 6 – Day 4

*Read John 16:5-15*

You may be wondering why on earth Valjean has come to the barricade. We have already mentioned that it was Cosette's blotter that had alerted him to her relationship with Marius. It was now Valjean's turn to be plunged into the darkness as he pondered a future without her.

*He had accepted every extremity when it had been necessary; he had sacrificed his inviolability as a reformed man, had yielded up his liberty, risked his head, lost everything, suffered everything, and he had remained disinterested and stoical to such a point that he might have been thought to be absent from himself like a martyr. His conscience inured to every assault of destiny, might have appeared to be forever impregnable. Well, anyone who had beheld his spiritual self would have been obliged to concede that it weakened at that moment. It was because, of all the tortures which he had undergone in the course of this long inquisition to which destiny had doomed him, this was the most terrible. ... Alas! The supreme trial, let us say rather, the only trial, is the loss of the beloved.*

In the early hours of the morning, Gavroche arrives in the Rue de L'Homme Arme. A sleepless Valjean is sitting on the curbstone outside the house. Eager to return to the action, Gavroche delivers Marius' letter to Valjean who reads it.

*Jean Valjean felt himself delivered. So he was about to find himself alone with Cosette once more. The rivalry would cease; the future was beginning again. He had but to keep this note in his pocket. Cosette would never know what had become of that man. All that there requires to be done is to let things take their own course. This man cannot escape. If he is not already dead, it is certain that he is about to die. What good fortune! Having said all this to himself, he became gloomy. Then he went down stairs and woke up the porter. About an hour later, Jean Valjean went out in the complete costume of a National Guard, and with his arms. The porter had easily found in the neighborhood the wherewithal to complete his equipment. He had a loaded gun and a cartridge-box filled with cartridges. He strode off in the direction of the markets.*

Valjean's problem seemed to have gone away as quickly as it arose so it is not thoughts of suicide that dictate his actions even if he does acknowledge to Javert that he doesn't expect to survive the night.

Death does indeed come to virtually everyone. Mabeuf is first to die, climbing to the top of the barricade to raise a standard and mown down by a hail of bullets.

Eponine dies taking a bullet that was aimed at Marius.

*She dropped her head again on Marius' knees, and her eyelids closed. He thought the poor soul had departed. Eponine remained motionless. All at once, at the very moment when Marius fancied her asleep forever, she slowly opened her eyes in which appeared the somber profundity of death, and said to him in a tone whose sweetness seemed already to proceed from another world: "And by the way, Monsieur Marius, I believe that I was a little bit in love with you." She tried to smile once more and expired.*

Gavroche makes his way back from the Rue de L'Homme Arme and dies fearlessly, recklessly even, collecting ammunition from the bodies of fallen soldiers in a striking contrast to his father's behavior at Waterloo.

One by one the students die. Last to die are Enjolras and Grantaire. Grantaire has been dead drunk for several hours and has missed the fighting. He wakes up just as Enjolras is about to be shot and elects to take a bullet with his hero.

Only two people survive – Valjean and Marius. They escape because Valjean has the presence of mind to pick up the unconscious body of the badly wounded Marius and carry it into the sewers.

Has Valjean decided that Marius is worthy of being reunited with Cosette? It is made clear to us that this is not the case either. As they pause in the sewer, we are told:

*Jean Valjean tore up his shirt, bandaged the young man's wounds as well as he was able and stopped the flowing blood; then bending over Marius, who still lay unconscious and almost without breathing, in that half light, he gazed at him with inexpressible hatred.*

So why has Valjean gone to the barricade? He has gone because once again he is following the voice of conscience. He has no idea from minute to minute how things will turn out but feels that he has no alternative. We have already considered the temptations of Jesus earlier in this study. At the beginning of that passage we are told that it was the Holy Spirit who led Jesus into the wilderness. The Greek word used does not suggest a mere option that Jesus might or might not take up. Rather it has the sense of compulsion – that Jesus was driven or even dragged into the wilderness. I guess that Jean Valjean would understand!

Today's Bible reading comes in the period between the Last Supper and Jesus' arrest. Jesus is preparing his disciples for their own personal time of darkness, his absence from them. He assures them that, even though he will not be there physically, they will be sent the Holy Spirit as a new companion. The Spirit will be the bridge between heaven and earth and will lead them just as he led Jesus. He will be their Counselor (or Comforter or Advocate or Helper or Strengthener or Encourager, depending on your Bible translation). Actually, the Greek word is παράκλητος (parakletòs) which means a person who comes alongside to support.

It's a wonderful picture. Even when we feel completely alone we know that he is there with us. We may feel daunted at the thought of sometimes being driven out of our own particular comfort zones but we can be assured that the Holy Spirit – the spirit of Jesus – is always by our side and on our side.

# Week 6 – Day 5

*Read John 12:12-16*

As Valjean carries the body of Marius through the stench and darkness of the sewers, a second drama is being played out above ground. Thenardier is being pursued along the banks of the Seine. His pursuer is Javert. For the second time in the book, Javert manages to lose a quarry just when he seems to have it cornered. This time the escape is not upward into the rarefied air of a convent but down into the hellhole of the sewer. Javert sits by the entrance and waits.

Meanwhile, Valjean is continuing his slow progress.

*This march became more and more laborious. The level of these vaults varies; the average height is about five feet, six inches, and has been calculated for the stature of a man; Jean Valjean was forced to bend over, in order not to strike Marius against the vault; at every step he had to bend, then to rise, and to feel incessantly of the wall. ... He stumbled along in the hideous dung heap of the city. ... Jean Valjean was both hungry and thirsty; especially thirsty; and this, like the sea, was a place full of water where a man cannot drink. His strength, which was prodigious, as the reader knows, and which had been but little decreased by age, thanks to his chaste and sober life, began to give way, nevertheless. Fatigue began to gain on him; and as his strength decreased, it made the weight of his burden increase. ... Between his legs he felt the rapid gliding of the rats. One of them was frightened to such a degree that it bit him.*

There are numerous partings of the way requiring decisions to be made. Worse still, there are stretches where the floor has given way, leaving excrement-filled quicksand underfoot. Valjean encounters just such a pit.

*Jean Valjean felt the pavement vanishing beneath his feet. He entered this slime. There was water on the surface, slime at the bottom. He must pass it. To retrace his steps was impossible. Marius was dying, and Jean Valjean exhausted. Besides, where was he to go? Jean Valjean advanced. Moreover, the pit seemed, for the first few steps, not to be very deep. But in proportion as he advanced, his feet plunged deeper. Soon he had the slime up to his calves and water above his knees. He walked on, raising Marius in his arms, as far above the water as he could. The mire now reached to his knees, and the water to his waist. He could no longer retreat. This mud, dense enough for one man, could not, obviously, uphold two. Marius and Jean Valjean would have stood a chance of extricating themselves singly. Jean Valjean continued to advance, supporting the dying man, who was, perhaps, a corpse. The water came up to his armpits; he felt that he was sinking; it was only with difficulty that he could move in the depth of ooze which he had now reached. The density, which was his support, was also an obstacle. He still held Marius on high, and with an unheard-of expenditure of force, he advanced still; but he was sinking. He had only his head above the water now and his two arms holding up Marius. In the old paintings of the deluge there is a mother holding her child thus. He sank still deeper, he turned his face to the rear, to escape the water, and in order that he might be able to breathe; anyone who had seen him in that gloom would have thought that what he beheld was a mask floating on the shadows; he caught a faint glimpse above him of the drooping head and livid face of Marius; he made a desperate effort and launched his foot forward; his foot struck something solid; a point of support. It was high time.*

Valjean finally comes to a grille but only to find that it is locked. At this point, he is joined by Thenardier who, not recognizing him under the slime, assumes him to be a murderer disposing of his victim's body. In return for a half-share of the little money that there is he produces a key and unlocks the grille. His motives are not entirely selfless. He is releasing Valjean into the arms of the waiting Javert.

For the second time in twenty-four hours, Valjean reveals his identity to Javert and allows himself to be taken into custody. He makes one request which is that, under Javert's supervision, he be allowed time to take Marius to his grandfather's house. This time the request is granted.

As the crowds flowed into Jerusalem for the Passover festival, Jesus rode into the city on a donkey. For those tuned into Old Testament prophecy it was the fulfillment of Zechariah 9. This speaks of a coming King who will be gentle and who will bring peace and salvation. As Jesus rode, the crowds waved palm branches and shouted many things including the chant 'Hosanna!' which means 'God save!'

And saving was exactly what Jesus had come to do even if it wasn't quite in the form that most of the crowd was looking for. Valjean saved Marius at the barricade. He carried him through the miry pit. His presence kept Marius from the demonic hands of Thenardier and from the prosecuting clutch of Javert. Without Valjean, any of those situations would have meant death for Marius. In the same way Jesus came to bring you salvation – from death, the depths of human experience, the Devil and the Law.

In Philippians, Paul speaks of Jesus having the nature of God but choosing to empty himself of all that glory and become nothing for our sake and for our salvation (Philippians 2). I like to think that Victor Hugo gives us a further dimension. He caused a minor stir when Les Misérables was published by including the word 'merde' (excrement or sh*t) in his description of the battle of Waterloo. One feels that it would have been so much more appropriate in his description of Valjean's saving grace, buried up to his nostrils in the 'dung heap of the city'.

Jesus did not just make himself nothing. He buried himself in the sh*t of human existence and he did it to save you!

# Week 6 – Day 6

*Read Matthew 11:11-15*

A year before the events of 1832, the Church of Scotland conducted a heresy trial against one of its ministers. John McLeod Campbell was expelled from the church for teaching that Jesus died on the cross for everyone, as opposed to the orthodox Calvinist position of his death being for a limited number of people – the elect. Campbell was never readmitted to the ministry of the Church but went on in 1856 to publish an important theological study entitled 'The Nature of the Atonement'.

Campbell's views were shaped in part by some thoughts of Martin Luther in his Commentary on Galatians. Discussing the thirteenth verse of Chapter 3 ("Christ hath redeemed us from the curse of the law, being made a curse for us: for it is written, cursed is every one that hangeth on a tree"), Luther commented that Jesus' death on the cross was a struggle between God's mercy and the anger of God as represented by the curse of the Law.

*"The curse of God waged a similar battle with the eternal mercy of God in Christ. The curse meant to condemn God's mercy. But it could not do it because the mercy of God is everlasting. The curse had to give way."*

Just such a battle is being played out in our story but inside Javert's head. After apprehending Valjean, Javert allows Marius to be delivered to his grandfather's house. He then instructs the carriage driver to go to the address that Valjean had given him at the barricade. Javert tells Valjean to go inside and that he will be waiting for his return but when Valjean looks out of a window, the street is empty. Javert has gone.

As we have seen previously, Javert has a complete faith in the law and a single-minded resolve as guardian of society to prosecute those who transgress. This is a role he sees as central to the maintenance of life, the universe and everything!

> *Without putting the thing clearly to himself, but with a confused intuition of the necessity of his presence and of his success, he, Javert, personified justice, light, and truth in their celestial function of crushing out evil. Behind him and around him, at an infinite distance, he had authority, reason, the case judged, the legal conscience, the public prosecution, all the stars; he was protecting order, he was causing the law to yield up its thunders, he was avenging society, he was lending a helping hand to the absolute, he was standing erect in the midst of a glory.*

Javert has no time for mercy as he reveals in the conversation with Valjean in which he asked to be dismissed from his post:

> *"Mr. Mayor, I do not desire that you should treat me kindly; your kindness roused sufficient bad blood in me when it was directed to others. I want none of it for myself. The kindness which consists in upholding a woman of the town against a citizen, the police agent against the mayor, the man who is down against the man who is up in the world, is what I call false kindness. That is the sort of kindness which disorganizes society. Good God! It is very easy to be kind; the difficulty lies in being just."*

Now Valjean's actions at the barricade, coupled with the reciprocal mercy that he has instinctively shown in return, have shattered his faith and plunged him into the darkness of mental torment. He perceives two seemingly impossible choices. The first is the path he knows. It is the demand of (the curse of) the Law. He should return to the house and arrest Valjean. But grace has opened his eyes to another possibility and this first option now seems detestable to him. The second path is the way of mercy – and also that of dereliction of his duty as a police inspector. And he sees still more.

Jesus describes John the Baptist as the greatest man ever born, which is no mean compliment! Yet John the Baptist belongs to the old order – the old covenant of law and prophets – and remarkably Jesus goes on to say that anyone who is part of the Kingdom of Heaven – the new covenant – is greater than John. (In case you missed it, that's you if you're a Christian!) This too is what Javert comes to perceive. As he reflects upon Valjean – his visible grace and his life as Madeleine – he experiences the same sensations that Valjean had, years previously, when confronted by the bishop. He sees the stature of Valjean, the convicted criminal, growing larger and larger whilst his own stature, the incorruptible upholder of the Law, is dwindling to nothing. It is the irresistible force meeting the previously immovable object. It is the iceberg meeting the *Titanic*. It is the revelation that the seemingly superhuman can turn out to have been subhuman.

Javert is experiencing the presence of God. He has touched upon a new world not based on the rigidity of law and punishment but on conscience, mercy and grace. It is a world that is indeed open not to a privileged few but to all. The greatest sadness is that it is also a world that can be viewed and rejected. God never forces himself upon anyone. God's mercy is sufficient to win you but not to keep you against your will.

Javert cannot cope nor can he see any way past the impasse. In the police force an inspector not wanting to follow orders can resign their post. Regrettably he decides that his only option is to resign from this new, higher authority.

Javert stands beside the Seine with the Palais de Justice and Notre Dame Cathedral – symbols of the old and new covenants – silhouetted in front of him:

*What lay below him was a void, so that he might have been standing at the edge of infinity. He stayed motionless for some minutes, staring into nothingness. Abruptly he took off his hat and laid it on the parapet. A moment later a tall, dark figure, which a passer-by might have taken for a ghost, stood upright on the parapet. It leaned forward and dropped into the darkness. There was a splash, and that was all.*

# Week 6 – Day 7

Questions for personal reflection or group discussion

Keyword for the week: Darkness

**Setting the scene**
Watch the DVD (17 minutes)
Start: Scene 15 The students preparing to fight (1:38:00)
Finish: Valjean nods to Enjolras (1:47:40)
Start: Scene 17 Javert standing in the street (1:57:59)
Finish: Javert's suicide (2:04:45)

**i 2 i**
*Issues to explore*
What stood out for you from this week's readings or movie clips?
Was there anything you didn't understand?
*Irritants*
Was there anything in the material with which you disagreed?

**The Day 6 Dilemma**
The struggle that comes from being a person created in the image
of God

What are Javert's good points and bad points?
    Three times Hugo pictures somebody coming face to face with
the grace of God in a person by using the image of increasing and
diminishing lights. Why do you think that Valjean (Week 1, Day
6) and Fantine (Week 3, Day 3) were enabled to respond to this
grace whereas Javert (Week 6, Day 6) was not? How might you
have responded in Javert's position?
    Do you see 'Javert' reflected in people that you know?

## Living it out

*Do not repay anyone evil for evil. Be careful to do what is right in the eyes of everyone. If it is possible, as far as it depends on you, live at peace with everyone. Do not take revenge, my dear friends, but leave room for God's wrath, for it is written: "It is mine to avenge; I will repay," says the Lord. On the contrary:*

*"If your enemy is hungry, feed him; if he is thirsty, give him something to drink. In doing this, you will heap burning coals on his head.*

*Do not be overcome by evil, but overcome evil with good."*
*(Romans 12:17-21)*

To seek blessing rather than revenge is not an easy thing to do. As Christians, where may we draw the strength to make this possible? How do the events of Holy Week help us?

Why are these verses even more difficult to follow in times of spiritual darkness?

Why may living at peace with others not depend on you? What can you do in such situations?

You might wish to look up some of the possible explanations for the phrase 'heap burning coals on your enemy's head'. Do you see this as a good or a bad thing?

Who do you see as your enemies?

### i 2 i

*Insights*
What insights have you gained from this week's material?
*Implementation*
Did you resolve to change anything in your life? What steps do you need to take to achieve this?

# 7

# Reconciliation

*He put an end to differences;*
*he prevented lawsuits, he reconciled enemies.*

## Week 7 – Day I

*Read Luke 15:11-24*

Gillenormand has been desperately waiting for his grandson to return home.

*At bottom, as we have said, M. Gillenormand idolized Marius. He idolized him after his own fashion, with an accompaniment of snappishness and boxes on the ear; but, this child once gone, he felt a black void in his heart; he would allow no one to mention the child to him, and all the while secretly regretted that he was so well obeyed. ... He never inquired about him, but he thought of him incessantly.*

Javert had informed the porter that they had brought a dead body but a doctor is called who confirms that Marius is still breathing. He has cuts to his head and arms – the exposed parts above the barricade – and a shattered shoulder blade. Only time will tell the severity of his head wounds and the depths of his unconsciousness, although he seems to have escaped serious injury. Gillenormand has not been informed but the noise wakes him. It is a great shock.

*"He is dead! He is dead! He is dead! He has got himself killed on the barricades! Out of hatred to me! He did that to spite me! Ah! You blood-drinker! This is the way he returns to me! Misery of my life, he is dead! ... Pierced, sabred, exterminated, slashed, hacked in pieces! Just look at that, the villain! He knew well that I was waiting for him, and that I had had his room arranged, and that I had placed at the head of my bed his portrait taken when he was a little child! He knew well that he had only to come back, and that I had been recalling him for years, and that I remained by my fireside, with my hands on my knees, not knowing what to do, and that I was mad*

*over it! You knew well, that you had but to return and to say: `It is I,' and you would have been the master of the house, and that I should have obeyed you, and that you could have done whatever you pleased with your old numskull of a grandfather! ... But you were pitiless in getting yourself killed like this, I shall not even grieve over your death, do you understand, you assassin?"*

*At that moment, Marius slowly opened his eyes, and his glance, still dimmed by lethargic wonder, rested on M. Gillenormand. "Marius!" cried the old man. "Marius! My little Marius! My child! My well-beloved son! You open your eyes, you gaze upon me, you are alive, thanks!" And he fell fainting.*

It takes six months but Marius is nursed back to health.

*At each succeeding phase of improvement, which became more and more pronounced, the grandfather raved. He executed a multitude of mechanical actions full of joy. He ascended and descended the stairs, without knowing why. A pretty female neighbor was amazed one morning to receive a big bouquet; it was M. Gillenormand who had sent it to her. The husband made a jealous scene. M. Gillenormand tried to draw Nicolette upon his knees. He called Marius, "M. le Baron." He shouted: "Long live the Republic!"*

Marius is also reunited with Cosette. Arrangements are made for their wedding which is to be on Shrove Tuesday and everybody is amazed when Valjean produces a dowry for Cosette amounting to nearly 600,000 francs. He also uses his experience of civil matters to smooth over Cosette's legal status and family background. Utilizing the convent years in which he had become Fauchelevent's 'brother', he maintains that the dead Fauchelevent is Cosette's father. The nuns of the convent had never enquired which Fauchelevent was the father. It hadn't interested them and they are happy to make the necessary declarations.

*Cosette became in the eyes of the law, Mademoiselle Euphrasie Fauchelevent. She was declared an orphan, both father and mother being dead. Jean Valjean so arranged it that he was appointed, under the name of Fauchelevent, as Cosette's guardian, with M. Gillenormand as supervising guardian over him.*

It has taken me a lifetime but I recently discovered pleonasms. For anyone still behind me on this one, a pleonasm is a phrase that uses more words than necessary for added effect. An example would be the expression 'safe haven'. My interest was sparked through reading the story of Zaccheus. Where the story, in English, speaks of Zaccheus running on ahead, the Greek uses a pleonasm – running ahead into the before.

The phrase also seems to fit the father of the lost son but with a double relevance. He has been desperately waiting for the moment his son returns home. Now that it's happened, he's not concerned with the appropriate decorum that should have applied to someone of his age and status. He hitches up his robes and he goes for it. He is running ahead into the before – running forward in the hope of restoring that which had previously been. Note too that the son's apology is not unimportant but the father's hug and kiss come first.

We are returning to a story in which we have previously cast Gillenormand as the younger son. Now he plays the father. What has changed? The answer is that time and absence have brought a sense of perspective. The political differences are still there. Dogma is still important but love has triumphed over dogma.

Jesus told the story to communicate something of his Father's love for us. It is never- ending. No matter how deeply we feel our guilt and shame and no matter how many times we may have made that journey home before, we will always find him running towards us with open arms. His heart has been yearning for our return.

A final word to earthly parents with absent children.

Sometimes like Gillenormand we wait and hope for their return but fail to communicate it. Maybe principles have got between us or we don't know what to say. Gillenormand thought that he'd blown it. Don't leave it too late because we don't all get second chances. You may not agree with them or with their behavior but it's never the wrong time to let someone know you love them and that they're welcome in your home.

# Week 7 – Day 2

*Read Luke 22:7-20*

It is Shrove Tuesday 1833 and it is Marius and Cosette's wedding day. It should be one of Valjean's finest hours. This is the girl who has filled his life for the last ten years. This is the girl he has protected, keeping the promise made to her mother. This is the girl he loves and without whom he has nothing of value in the whole world. Yet, as the guests sit down to their wedding meal, he is absent.

For several days, Jean Valjean has had his arm in a sling. It has meant that he has been unable to sign the marriage documents as Cosette's guardian and so Gillenormand has deputized for him. Pleading the need to rest, he excuses himself from the ongoing festivities. The truth is that he is about to face his greatest trial.

Some people will claim that to be a Christian is to be prosperous. It could well be argued that Christian values and discipline are more likely to result in prosperity but God does not call us to be prosperous. He calls us to be faithful, from which prosperity may or may not be a by-product. If conscience comes calling then prosperity must go packing if the two are in conflict. There can be no alternative. The one must be sacrificed to the other.

The story is told of a millionaire who was asked to return to his home church and speak to the Sunday school. He told the children of the day when he had been sitting where they were with a penny in his pocket. He felt that God had been telling him to give up his penny, which was all the money that he had in the world. "I gave up all that I had", he said, "and look how God has rewarded me since." At which point a voice piped up – "I dare you to do it again." Valjean has already been asked that question in revealing his identity at Arras and his white hair is testimony to the violence of the struggle. Now the question is being asked of him again but the stakes have multiplied immeasurably.

Jesus was celebrating the Passover with his disciples. Anyone who has shared in a Passover meal will know that it is a time of great jollity and celebration. It recalls both the release of the Israelites from slavery in Egypt into the Promised Land and their place as God's chosen people. It is an evening to which, Jesus says, he has been looking forward, an opportunity to share with his closest friends. And yet this happy occasion too has an edge of sadness to it. Jesus is having to face up to his ultimate trial. Soon he will be asked to make the greatest sacrifice of his life and of the life of the world.

He reclines at table and prepares them for a Kingdom – his Kingdom – to which he must soon return. He breaks the bread and prepares them for a broken body – his body – hung up on a cross. He blesses the wine and prepares them for blood – his blood – soon to be spilt. And after the meal, he retires to the Mount of Olives to pray the night away.

The sacrifice that Valjean's conscience is asking him to make is no less demanding than that asked of his master. It is very simple. Cosette no longer needs his protection. He is an escaped convict who will be returned to jail if caught. If this happens it will bring disgrace and shame to Cosette and Marius. As he does not in any way wish to mar their happiness, the only answer is to begin distancing himself from Cosette. When the separation is complete no harm will be able to come to her. This is also the reason for the sling. There is no injury but the signature on the documents of a convict – a non-person – might have rendered the marriage invalid.

And like Jesus before him, Valjean spends a long night agonizing over what might lie ahead. Beside him on the bed he lays the few objects that he has retained wherever they have travelled but which nobody else has seen. These are the first clothes in which he dressed Cosette after rescuing her from the hell of Montfermeil.

Cosette, that charming existence, was the raft of this shipwreck. What was he to do? To cling fast to it, or to let go his hold? If he clung to it, he should emerge from disaster, he should ascend again into the sunlight, he should let the bitter water drip from his garments and his hair, he was saved, he should live. And if he let go his hold? Then the abyss. Thus he took sad council with his thoughts. Or, to speak more correctly, he fought; he kicked furiously internally, now against his will, now against his conviction. ... At length, Jean Valjean entered into the peace of exhaustion. He weighed, he reflected, he considered the alternatives, the mysterious balance of light and darkness. Should he impose his galleys on those two dazzling children, or should he consummate his irremediable engulfment by himself? On one side lay the sacrifice of Cosette, on the other that of himself.

... He remained there until daylight, in the same attitude, bent double over that bed, prostrate beneath the enormity of fate, crushed, perchance, alas! with clenched fists, with arms outspread at right angles, like a man crucified who has been un-nailed, and flung face down on the earth. There he remained for twelve hours, the twelve long hours of a long winter's night, ice-cold, without once raising his head, and without uttering a word. ... Anyone to behold him thus motionless would have pronounced him dead; all at once he shuddered convulsively, and his mouth, glued to Cosette's garments, kissed them; then it could be seen that he was alive.

Who could see? Since Jean Valjean was alone, and there was no one there.

The One who is in the shadows.

# Week 7 – Day 3

*Read Matthew 27:45-50*

The day after the wedding, Valjean asks to see Marius in private. We remind ourselves that he is an escaped criminal under sentence and does not want his crimes to bring a stain to Cosette's name. Valjean has come to a decision.

He reveals his secret to Marius who is staggered but protests that they could still live as one family. Valjean does not see it that way.

> *As one family! No. I belong to no family. I do not belong to yours. I do not belong to any family of men. In houses where people are among themselves, I am superfluous. There are families, but there is nothing of the sort for me. I am an unlucky wretch; I am left outside. Did I have a father and mother? I almost doubt it.*
>
> *On the day when I gave that child in marriage, all came to an end. I have seen her happy, and that she is with a man whom she loves, and that there exists here a kind old man, a household of two angels, and all joys in that house, and that it was well, I said to myself: 'Enter thou not.' I could have lied, it is true, have deceived you all, and remained Monsieur Fauchelevent. So long as it was for her, I could lie; but now it would be for myself, and I must not. It was sufficient for me to hold my peace, it is true, and all would go on. You ask me what has forced me to speak? a very odd thing; my conscience. To hold my peace was very easy, however. I passed the night in trying to persuade myself to it ... You ask why I speak? I am neither denounced, nor pursued, nor tracked, you say. Yes! I am denounced! Yes! I am tracked! By whom? By myself. It is I who bar the passage to myself, and I drag myself, and I push myself, and I arrest myself, and I execute myself, and when one holds oneself, one is firmly held."*
>
> *And, seizing a handful of his own coat by the nape of the neck and extending it towards Marius:*

*"Do you see that fist?"* he continued. *"Don't you think that it holds that collar in such a wise as not to release it? Well! Conscience is another grasp! If one desires to be happy, sir, one must never understand duty; for, as soon as one has comprehended it, it is implacable. One would say that it punished you for comprehending it; but no, it rewards you; for it places you in a hell, where you feel God beside you. One has no sooner lacerated his own entrails than he is at peace with himself."*

The title of the chapter in which these events occur is 'The Seventh Circle and the Eighth Heaven'. It is a reference to Dante's *Divine Comedy*. The Seventh Circle is one of the lowest points in Hell where sinners are tormented for their crimes. The Eighth Heaven is very close to the seat of God, only just short of the angels. This is Valjean's torture through the prompting of his conscience. If he is to see the face of God he must put himself through the depths of hell.

It is agreed that it would indeed be best if Valjean does not see Cosette again but as he is about to leave he asks Marius to reconsider.

*"If you will allow it, I will come to see her. I assure you that I desire it greatly. If I had not cared to see Cosette, I should not have made to you the confession that I have made, I should have gone away; but, as I desired to remain in the place where Cosette is, and to continue to see her, I had to tell you about it honestly. You follow my reasoning, do you not? It is a matter easily understood. You see, I have had her with me for more than nine years. We lived first in that hut on the boulevard, then in the convent, then near the Luxembourg. That was where you saw her for the first time. You remember her blue plush hat. Then we went to the Quartier des Invalides, where there was a railing on a garden, the Rue Plumet. I lived in a little back courtyard, whence I could hear her piano. That was my life. We never left each other. That lasted for nine years and*

*some months. I was like her own father, and she was my child. I do not know whether you understand, Monsieur Pontmercy, but to go away now, never to see her again, never to speak to her again, to no longer have anything, would be hard. If you do not disapprove of it, I will come to see Cosette from time to time. I will not come often. I will not remain long. ... What I can do, by the way, is to come in the afternoon, when night is beginning to fall."*

Marius grants Valjean's request and says that he may come every evening.

It is a final act of love. Valjean goes through hell in order to protect the purity of Cosette's name. He cuts himself adrift in order that the judgment on his former life should have no effect upon her.

Imagine somebody doing that in order to protect the purity of your name and reputation, only it wasn't their own crimes that they were bearing but yours. Imagine that they were protecting you not from the negative implications of their own actions but from the things that you had done.

Peter uses the prophecy of Isaiah to describe what Jesus did for us on the cross.

*He never sinned, nor ever deceived anyone. He did not retaliate when he was insulted, nor threaten revenge when he suffered. He left his case in the hands of God, who always judges fairly. He personally carried our sins in his body on the cross so that we can be dead to sin and live for what is right. By his wounds you are healed.* (1 Peter 2:22-24 NLT)

On the cross Jesus carried your sins and those of the whole world, past, present and future. He died for you. He went through hell for you. And for you he cried, "My God, my God, why have you forsaken me?", cut off by your sins from the one person whom he loved the most.

# Week 7 – Day 4

*Read John 19:25-27*

As Marius reflects upon his conversation with Valjean he begins to have second thoughts and regrets having agreed to let him see Cosette. Marius is no Javert but for a would-be revolutionary his thoughts are still very conservative.

> *But do what he would, and seek what extenuation he would, he was certainly forced to fall back upon this: the man was a convict; that is to say, a being who has not even a place in the social ladder, since he is lower than the very lowest rung. After the very last of men comes the convict. The convict is no longer, so to speak, in the semblance of the living. The law has deprived him of the entire quantity of humanity of which it can deprive a man. ... In this stage of his ideas, Jean Valjean appeared to him hideous and repulsive. He was a man reproved, he was the convict. That word was for him like the sound of the trump on the Day of Judgment; and, after having reflected upon Jean Valjean for a long time, his final gesture had been to turn away his head.*

Two further thoughts repulse him. He had personally seen (or thought he had) Valjean murder Javert in what he now presumes to have been some sort of revenge attack. His enquiries have also revealed the disappearance of more than 600,000 francs of Madeleine's money from Montreuil-Sur-Mer. His assumption is that Valjean and Madeleine had at one time been fellow convicts and that Valjean has killed Madeleine for his money.

Marius does not intend to break his promise to Valjean so instead sets out to communicate that he is not welcome after all. On Valjean's first visit he is provided with a basement room in which to see Cosette. A little after this, Marius gives instructions that the fire in the room not be lit. The fire is relit after Cosette protests but the chairs are moved to the other end of the room. Then they are removed altogether. Cosette is so absorbed by the delights of marriage that she is oblivious to what's really going on.

Cosette also mentions to Valjean that something has puzzled her. Marius has asked whether she thinks they can get by without touching the dowry. The message is clear to Valjean if not to Cosette. Marius now regards the dowry to be tainted money.

Realizing that Marius has changed his mind, Valjean makes the painful decision to stop coming.

*On the following day he did not come. Cosette only observed the fact in the evening. "Why," said she, "Monsieur Jean has not been here today." And she felt a slight twinge at her heart, but she hardly perceived it, being immediately diverted by a kiss from Marius. On the following day he did not come. Cosette paid no heed to this, passed her evening and slept well that night, as usual, and thought of it only when she woke. She was so happy! She speedily dispatched Nicolette to M. Jean's house to inquire whether he was ill, and why he had not come on the previous evening. Nicolette brought back the reply of M. Jean that he was not ill. He was busy. He would come soon. As soon as he was able. Moreover, he was on the point of taking a little journey. Madame must remember that it was his custom to take trips from time to time. They were not to worry about him. They were not to think of him.*

Bereft of the one thing he cares about in the world, Valjean goes into a rapid downward spiral. He stops eating and gives up the will to live. Whenever Cosette sends messages to the house asking whether he has returned, he returns a message that he has not. At twilight each day he makes a slow pilgrimage towards Cosette's street.

*... he reached the Rue des Filles-du-Calvaire; then he halted, he trembled, he thrust his head with a sort of melancholy timidity round the corner of the last house, and gazed into that street, and there was in that tragic look something which resembled the dazzling light of the impossible, and the reflection from a paradise that was closed to him. Then a tear, which had slowly gathered in the corner of his lids, and had become large enough to fall, trickled down his cheek, and sometimes stopped at his mouth. The old man tasted its bitter flavor.*

As Valjean's strength fails, he is reduced to his rooms and then to his bed. He is fading fast. He tries to write a final letter explaining the probity of the dowry but the pen slips from his fingers before he can finish. The end is approaching and his greatest distress is that he will never see Cosette again.

*"It is nothing to die, what is frightful is to die without seeing her. She would smile on me, she would say a word to me, would that do any harm to any one? No, all is over, and forever. Here I am all alone. My God! My God! I shall never see her again!"*

It is a strange but true fact that we can bear insults, deprivations and torments far more easily when they are directed towards ourselves than when they are happening to people dear to us. Ask any parent of grown-up children for starters. It is our worst nightmare to care for but be unable to help the ones we love.

It must have been agony for Mary but imagine too, the pain for Jesus as he looked down from the cross. There was the physical pain he was enduring but there was also the emotional pain. As he looked down at his mother, his family and his friends, there was nothing he could do for them anymore. He was separated from them and, in a short while, that separation would be permanent. All he was able to do was to ask John (who may have been his cousin) to take over his responsibility as eldest son of a widow. It is not something that we usually think about but Jesus' heart must have been breaking just as much as Valjean's heart was breaking at the loss of Cosette.

## Week 7 – Day 5

*Read John 17:20-26*

On the same day that Jean Valjean despairs of ever seeing Cosette again, Marius receives a letter and an accompanying visitor. The letter comes from a familiar hand:

> *Monsieur le Baron: If the Supreme Being had given me the talents, I might have been baron Thenard, member of the Institute* [academy of sciences], *but I am not. I only bear the same as him, happy if this memory recommends me to the eccellence of your kindnesses. The benefit with which you will honor me will be reciprocle.*
>
> *I am in possession of a secret concerning an individual. This individual concerns you. I hold the secret at your disposal desiring to have the honor to be huseful to you. I will furnish you with the simple means of driving from your honorabel family that individual who has no right there, madame la baronne being of lofty birth. The sanctuary of virtue cannot cohabit longer with crime without abdicating.*
>
> *I awate in the entichamber the orders of monsieur le baron.*
>
> *With respect,*
>
> *The letter was signed Thenard.*

The writer is, of course, Thenardier who has realized that Valjean was the 'murderer' in the sewer and is seeking to sell this information. Marius sees straight through his alias and proceeds to tell him that he already knows that Valjean is an ex-convict whom he believes to be responsible for the murders of Madeleine and Javert. For the second time, Thenardier inadvertently comes to Valjean's aid. Before revealing his own news he corrects Marius. He shows, with the help of newspaper clippings, that Valjean and Madeleine were indeed the same person and that Javert committed suicide. Marius is dumbstruck. He now realizes that

Valjean is someone truly worthy of veneration but there is more to come.

As Thenardier reveals the 'truth' about Valjean and his victim in the sewer, he produces a piece of material that he had cut from the young man's jacket and kept as evidence. It matches a hole in Marius' jacket and shows him that it was Valjean who was the savior that had brought him home.

The cross was supposed to be an end. The soldiers banged in the nails. The leaders thought themselves rid of a thorn in their side. The theologians reasoned that God would not allow any son of his to bear the curse of crucifixion. The scoffers scoffed. Like Thenardier they came to bury a man's reputation. Like Thenardier they saw it spectacularly backfire.

On the third day, we stare open-mouthed into an open-mouthed tomb. It is empty. All that evil has done is reveal the truth. Truly this was the Son of God, to be worshipped and adored. Truly this is my savior.

Marius and Cosette rush to Valjean. They are just in time. He is dying. Lit candles adorn the bishop's candlesticks on the mantelpiece. Valjean asks Cosette to keep them.

*"They are of silver, but to me they are gold … I do not know whether the person who gave them to me is pleased with me yonder on high. I have done what I could. My children, you will not forget that I am a poor man; you will have me buried in the first plot of earth that you find, under a stone to mark the spot. This is my wish. No name on the stone. … Do you remember Montfermeil, Cosette? You were in the woods, and you were frightened. I helped you carry the bucket, do you remember? That was the first time I touched your poor hand. It was so cold! Your hands were red in those days, Mademoiselle, and now they are white. And do you remember that big doll? You called her Catherine, and you wished you could have taken her to the convent. You made me laugh at times, angel that you were."*

Valjean's final advice to Marius and Cosette is that they 'love one another always' because 'there is nothing else that matters in this world except love'. He is taking the baton that he received from Bishop Myriel and passing it on to the next generation.

Likewise, today's reading contains John's record of the final words spoken by Jesus before his arrest and crucifixion. Jesus is praying for the church that will develop from the post-resurrection witness of the disciples and which includes you and me. He prays that we may have unity, a unity of heart and mind both with each other and with him. This is not just for ourselves. In so doing we serve as a witness to the world of the redeeming presence of Jesus and a tangible outworking of his love.

This is our crusade. We serve a resurrected King. We take up his baton of love and grace and, empowered by his Spirit, continue to work towards a Kingdom that gives sanctuary to both the physical and the spiritual *misérables* of the world.

*"Will you join in our crusade? Who will be strong and stand with me?"*

That challenge comes from the song *Do You Hear the People Sing?* and owes much to Herbert Kretzmer's translation of the original French *Les Misérables* lyrics. The song both opens and closes the second act of the musical yet each appearance is very different. In its first outing, it's a song of rebellion as the students prepare for battle. Being strong, here, has to do with barricades; with angry men; with the blood of martyrs. By the finale, all this has changed. Talk of violence has gone. In its place is a biblical vision of a light that can never be extinguished and the promise of a new day where swords will give way to plowshares and all chains of bondage will be broken. It has become a picture of a God-reconciled world, the very same that Jesus himself was envisioning and towards which he invites our commitment.

*"Will you join in our crusade? Who will be strong and stand with me?"*

Will you?

To quote Jesus: I have come that they may have life, and have it to the full.

To quote Jean Valjean: To die is nothing; but it is terrible not to live.

# Week 7 – Day 6

## Postscript

*Read John 21:15-19*

You've made it through to the final day of reading, which is more than can be said for most of the book's characters. It's a regular complaint that just about anyone you might care about in *Les Misérables* gets killed off. Even the ending, where the wedding of Cosette and Marius could have made a fitting finale, is marred by the seemingly needless death of Valjean. Why is the misery so unrelenting?

Three things need to be said. Firstly, to remind ourselves that Victor Hugo's purpose was to highlight the plight of the poor. For them there is usually no happy ending. The misery is indeed unrelenting. Secondly, it is worth recalling that God does not immunize the Christian from the suffering of life but promises we shall find him in its midst, transforming from the inside. For the Greeks, the ideal was that of the gods on Mount Olympus. They were removed from suffering – literally απαθεια (apatheia = without suffering). It's the root of the English word apathy because to be removed from suffering is also to be disengaged. That was not Jesus' goal in life or death. Neither is it ours.

And, thirdly, we miss something crucial if we fail to see that it is sacrifice and martyrdom that underpin the key moments in *Les Misérables*. The actions of Bishop Myriel and Georges Pontmercy in giving up precious possessions – the candlesticks and Marius – define the two halves of the story. Pure Sister Simplice lies *twice in succession, one after the other, without hesitation, promptly, as a person does when sacrificing herself*. Gavroche, Eponine and Mabeuf are all portrayed as consciously sacrificing their lives. So too the students, who *give their life a free offering to progress; they accomplish the will of providence; they perform a religious act*. Even Javert, if you take his inflexibility to mean that suicide is the only way he can preserve Valjean's freedom.

The greatest expressions of martyrdom, though, belong with Fantine and Valjean. As Fantine's life is ebbing away, forfeited for Cosette, her martyr status is underscored.

> She drew aside the curtain and saw M. Madeleine standing there and looking at something over her head. His gaze was full of pity, anguish, and supplication. She followed its direction, and saw that it was fixed on a crucifix which was nailed to the wall. ... At last she said timidly: "What are you doing?" ... "I was praying to the martyr there on high." And he added in his own mind, "For the martyr here below."

The same idea returns in Valjean's death scene:

> All at once he rose to his feet. These accesses of strength are sometimes the sign of the death agony. He walked with a firm step to the wall, thrusting aside Marius and the doctor who tried to help him, detached from the wall a little copper crucifix which was suspended there, and returned to his seat with all the freedom of movement of perfect health, and said in a loud voice, as he laid the crucifix on the table: "Behold the great martyr."

Again we are left with double meaning. There is a great martyr above and below. You may not like Valjean's demise but it is consistent with Victor Hugo's grand plan.

Why is this theme so important for Hugo? In part, he is reflecting a strand of nineteenth-century French Catholicism that saw suffering, if voluntarily embraced, as being redemptive for the world. There is no time to pursue this here but if you want to explore further then read up on the life and popular acclaim of St. Therese of Lisieux (1873-1897) who, like Fantine, died of tuberculosis in her twenties. More than this, though, Hugo is stating a simple truth. Lasting change is rarely achieved through force and violence. Barricades only separate. Instead, we follow the example of one who, in his self-sacrifice, has broken down the walls that divide (Ephesians 2:14).

Today's reading is often titled "The Restoration of Peter". Peter, in the garden of Gethsemane, has spectacularly lost the plot and sliced off a man's ear in trying to forcibly protect Jesus from arrest. He then undertakes a reconnaissance mission behind enemy lines that results only in him denying Jesus three times. You can imagine how he is feeling. Now comes the moment of reconciliation. Jesus encourages him to reaffirm his love, in triplicate, once for each of the denials. The renewed relationship carries a cost, martyrdom, and a continuing responsibility to feed others with the life and love of Jesus. The man who would live by the sword has to learn that far more can be gained when he is prepared, non-violently, to die by it.

Chapter 21, though, might seem a strange ending for John's Gospel. Like Victor Hugo, John appears unable to quit whilst ahead. Wouldn't the previous chapter have made a more powerful conclusion? The stone has been rolled away; the empty tomb discovered. The resurrected Jesus appears to Mary and then breathes his empowering Spirit into the cowered disciples. Thomas, allowed a rerun, acknowledges Jesus as "My Lord and my God!" And John concludes that Thomas is intended to stand for us all. His stated hope is that *"You may believe that Jesus is the Christ, the Son of God, and that by believing you may have life in his name."*

Instead of finishing there, John adds this extra chapter focused not so much on the glorious deeds of Jesus as sorting out the inglorious deeds of Peter. Isn't it a mistake? Surely an editor would have advised John to quit on a high.

It's no mistake. Chapter 21 completes Chapter 20. As Paul tells the Corinthians, *"God was reconciling the world to himself in Christ, not counting people's sins against them."* This is the big picture stuff that comes to glorious fulfillment in John 20. This is why Jesus journeyed to the cross. But Paul goes on. The nuts and bolts of reconciliation, modeled for us by Jesus with Peter, have to be followed through in real time. *"And he has committed to us the message of reconciliation. We are therefore Christ's ambassadors, as though God were making his appeal through us"* (2 Corinthians 5:19-20). The journey continues.

The big picture Jesus of the resurrection executes the fine detail, performing the miracle of reconciliation first for Peter and, since then, in countless individual lives. He does it with the help of anyone willing to be his ambassador – a bishop here; an ex-con there; and the likes of you and me.

# Week 7 – Day 7

Questions for personal reflection or group discussion

Keyword for the week: Reconciliation

**Setting the scene**
Watch the DVD (17 minutes)
Start: Scene 18 Marius in bed (2:04:45)
Finish: "To love another person is to see the face of God" (2:21:48)

**i 2 i**
*Issues to explore*
What stood out for you from this week's readings or movie clip?
Was there anything you didn't understand?
*Irritants*
Was there anything in the material with which you disagreed?

**The Day 6 Dilemma**
The struggle that comes from being a person created in the image
of God

Remind yourself of those moments when the book's characters
have to make sacrificial choices. Do you ever count the cost of
your commitment in terms of sacrifice or even possible
martyrdom? How might the image of Jesus breathing the Holy
Spirit into fearful disciples (John 20) help in such a situation?

Read 2 Corinthians 5:18-21. What do you understand by the
'message of reconciliation'? Is it just spiritual? Or does it have a
social dimension? An emotional dimension? An environmental
dimension? Some other?

Do you feel that you are helping Jesus in his work of reconciliation or doing his work for him? Is the difference significant?

## Living it out

*Bless those who persecute you; bless and do not curse. Rejoice with those who rejoice; mourn with those who mourn. Live in harmony with one another. Do not be proud, but be willing to associate with people of low position. Do not be conceited. (Romans 12:14-16)*

Living in harmony with others necessarily means breaking down the mental barriers that divide *us* from *them*. The following obstacles are suggested from these verses.

- Enmity and bitterness

- Jealousy and envy that can stop us rejoicing with others

- Lack of compassion and understanding that can stop us mourning with others

- Pride in our social standing

- Pride in our supposed intellectual superiority

How powerful are these factors in your life? Would you add any others?

How easy is it to carry God's message of reconciliation to others if you are not reconciled to them yourself?

The word reconciliation suggests a restoration of a pre-existing relationship. It can also have a technical meaning used when a previously disused church is rededicated to God. Is it helpful to see our mission in these terms that, through deeds and words, we are inviting people back to the lives for which God originally created them? Is anybody beyond God's message of reconciliation?

## Watch the DVD

(2 minutes)

Start: "To love another person is to see the face of God" (2:21:48)

Finish: Closing credits

Reflect for a few moments upon some of the characters whose journeys you have shared over the past few weeks. Which have touched you the most? Do you feel particularly drawn to any of their situations? Could this suggest possible ways in which God might want to use you/your group/your church?

- Valjean – The ex-prisoner who discovers that most of society is still weighted heavily against him.

- Fantine – The single parent making huge sacrifices for her child and going under.

- Young Cosette – The child that needs liberating from an abusive relationship.

- Mabeuf – The pensioner that has worked hard all his live but now struggles to get by on meager means.

- Eponine – The teenager exposed to terrible parental role models but with potential that could be developed by an appropriate mentor.

- Gavroche – The young person with plenty of energy and passion. Amazing if it could be channeled in the right directions.

- The younger Thenardier boys – Out on the street and vulnerable.

**i 2 i**

*Insights*

What insights have you gained from the course?

*Implementation*

Did you resolve to change anything in your life? What steps do you need to take to achieve this?

# Who's who in *Les Misérables*

A list of characters featured in this book.

Warning: Contains spoilers.

**Bahorel**: Member of the ABC group of Parisian student revolutionaries.

**Monseigneur Bienvenu**: (Lit. Monseigneur Welcome) An alternative name for Bishop Myriel.

**Blachevelle**: Boyfriend of Favourite; one of Fantine's group of friends in Paris.

**Champmathieu**: Peasant with a strong resemblance to Jean Valjean who is tried in a case of mistaken identity.

**Combeferre**: Member of the ABC group of Parisian student revolutionaries.

**Cosette**: Daughter of Fantine; Cosette is a nickname as her real name is Euphrasie. Brought up by Valjean after her mother's death.

**Courfeyrac**: Member of the ABC group of Parisian student revolutionaries.

**Dahlia**: Girlfriend of Listolier; one of Fantine's group of friends in Paris.

**Enjolras**: Leader of the ABC group of Parisian student revolutionaries.

**Fameuil**: Boyfriend of Zephine; one of Fantine's group of friends in Paris.

**Fantine**: Orphan whose relationship with a Parisian student leaves her with a child, Cosette. She is never given a surname.

**Monsieur Fauchelevent**: An elderly man fallen on hard times whom Valjean rescues from underneath his upturned cart. He later reappears as the gardener at the Petit-Picpus convent in Paris which enables Valjean and Cosette to find sanctuary there.

**Ultime Fauchelevent**: An alias used by Jean Valjean whilst living in Paris.

**Favourite**: Girlfriend of Blachevelle; one of Fantine's group of friends in Paris.

**Feuilly**: Member of the ABC group of Parisian student revolutionaries.

**Monsieur Gillenormand**: Marius' grandfather who is completely opposed to his political views. He appears only fleetingly in the movie and not at all in the musical.

**Grantaire**: Member of the ABC group of Parisian student revolutionaries.

**Inspector Javert**: Police inspector who is Jean Valjean's nemesis throughout the novel. He is never given a Christian name.

**Joly**: Member of the ABC group of Parisian student revolutionaries.

**General Jean Maximilien Lamarque**: Real-life commander of the French army under Napoleon and member of the French Parliament. Lamarque's funeral did spark a short-lived insurrection in June 1832, around which Victor Hugo created his fictional account.

**Lesgle**: Member of the ABC group of Parisian student revolutionaries.

**Listolier**: Boyfriend of Dahlia; one of Fantine's group of friends in Paris.

**Monsieur Mabeuf**: Impoverished Parisian author whom we first meet as the churchwarden who reveals to Marius the truth about his father. He does not appear in the musical or movie.

**Monsieur Madeleine**: An alias used by Jean Valjean whilst living in Montreuil-Sur-Mer.

**Bishop Charles François Bienvenu Myriel**: Bishop of Digne whose generosity enables Jean Valjean to reform his life.

**Nicolette:** Maid serving Monsieur Gillenormand's household.

**Patron-Minette**: Small band of Parisian criminals associated with the Thenardiers.

**Georges Pontmercy**: Father of Marius and veteran of the Battle of Waterloo where he believes (wrongly) that Thenardier saved his life. He does not appear in the musical or movie in which Marius has no back story.

**Marius Pontmercy**: Parisian student revolutionary and love interest for Cosette.

**Jean Prouvaire**: Member of the ABC group of Parisian student revolutionaries.

**Sister Perpetua and Sister Simplice**: Nuns who tend to Fantine in hospital. Sister Simplice is renowned for her absolute truthfulness. Her actions play a pivotal role in the book but do not feature in the musical or movie.

**Thenardier and Madame Thenardier**: Criminally minded individuals whom we first meet as innkeepers at Montfermeil and who are never given Christian names. Parents to Azelma, Eponine, Gavroche and two further unnamed boys. They are also known by the aliases Jondrette and Thenard.

**Azelma Thenardier**: Daughter of the Thenardiers who does not appear in the musical or movie.

**Eponine Thenardier**: Daughter of the Thenardiers; has a crush on Marius.

**Gavroche Thenardier**: Oldest of the Thenardiers' sons who, in Paris, lives on the streets and in a giant wood and plaster elephant left over from the end of the Napoleonic era. In the musical and movie, there is no mention of his connection to the Thenardier family.

**Felix Tholomyes**: Parisian student who abandons Fantine leaving her with a young child. He does not appear in the musical or movie where the inference is given (wrongly) that she was deserted whilst pregnant.

**Jean Valjean**: Reformed convict whose struggles, on the run from the law, form the basis of the story.

**Madame Victurnien**: 'Christian' busybody whose actions lead to Fantine losing her employment which begins a slide towards prostitution. She does not appear in the musical or movie where Fantine's 'secret' is discovered inside the factory rather than outside.

**Zephine**: Girlfriend of Fameuil; one of Fantine's group of friends in Paris.